JAPANESE SUPER CARS

JAPANESE
SUPER
CARS

TERRY JACKSON

MALLARD
PRESS

MALLARD PRESS

An imprint of BDD Promotional
Book Company, Inc.
666 Fifth Avenue, New York, NY 10103

Mallard Press and its accompanying
design and logo are trademarks of
BDD Promotional Book Company, Inc.

First published in the United States of America
in 1992 by the Mallard Press

ISBN 0-7924-5730-7

This book was designed and produced by
Quintet Publishing Limited
6 Blundell Street
London N7 9BH

Creative Director: Richard Dewing
Designer: Chris Dymond
Project Editors: Stefanie Foster, Lindsay Porter
Editor: Rosemary Booton

Typeset in Great Britain by
Central Southern Typesetters, Eastbourne
Manufactured in Hong Kong by
Regent Publishing Services Limited
Printed in Hong Kong by
Leefung-Asco Printers Limited

Contents

日本のスポーツッカー

M y first exposure to Japanese sports cars was both startling and a prediction of the future. There was a small, two-room garage near my boyhood home in Baltimore, Maryland, that catered to a significant contingent of local sports car owners. On any given day, the place was littered with MGs, Triumphs, Sunbeams, Austin-Healeys, Jaguars and even a Ferrari or two.

One of the regulars was a professor at Johns Hopkins University who owned a 1967 XKE coupé. Although the E-Type was this man's pride and joy, it was also the bane of his motoring life. He had a constant litany of complaints, from electrical problems to the engine overheating. But he was also committed to the marque, this being his third Jaguar in 10 years. Then one day in late 1969, he arrived at the garage in a new car, a sleek two-seater coupé unlike any I had ever seen. The professor got out of the coupé and introduced us to what he called the sports car of the future – the Datsun 240Z.

The purists in our little group laughed at the idea of a Japanese sports car, but the 240Z – with its 150-horsepower in-line 2.4-litre six, its MacPherson strut suspension, its all-synchromesh four-speed gearbox and its exceptional fit and finish – proved us wrong. It had all the attributes of European sports cars and few of the vices. In fact, though the professor would often stop at the garage for coffee, he never had to visit because the 240Z needed repairing – unlike when he owned his Jaguar.

More than 155,000 Datsun Zs were sold in its first three years, establishing Datsun – known today as Nissan – as a serious sports car builder. The success of the 240Z was a breakthrough for Japanese manufacturers, the culmination of more than a decade of tentative yet significant efforts to create world-class sports cars.

Datsun was the first Rising Sun manufacturer to build a viable, yet still crude, sports car in 1959 with its Fairlady S211 two-seater roadster –

BELOW: The 2.4-litre in-line six engine was the basis for the name 240Z.

LEFT: Attractively styled, very reliable and powerful for its day, the Datsun 240Z was a milestone car when it was introduced.

named for the popular stage musical, *My Fair Lady*. This car was cast in the British sports car mould, but it was not well done and few examples were exported from Japan.

A more serious effort came in 1962, when Datsun introduced its answer to the MGB, the Fairlady SPL 310 (known in the United States as the Datsun 1500 roadster). Powered by a four-cylinder, 85-horsepower engine, the SPL 310 was a serious, though little known, sports car contender. Undaunted and with an intense desire to improve, Datsun upgraded the 1500 in 1965 with the 1600 Sports, which was more powerful and more refined. Engine size was increased to 1600cc, a near-perfect four-speed gearbox was added, as were front-wheel disc brakes. The interior was dressed up considerably, and the base price of $2,621 made it quite a bargain – another key Japanese strategy.

In 1967, Datsun made more significant improvements to its two-seater sports car when it introduced the 2000 Sports, which had a two-litre overhead camshaft, four-cylinder 135-horsepower engine and, for the era, the daring innovation of a five-speed overdrive gearbox. The

LEFT: Spoked wheel covers helped keep the price of the 240Z at an affordable level.

BOTTOM: Datsun's peppy 1600 convertible was the forerunner of the 240Z.

BELOW: Z-car emblem against the Japanese flag was a symbol that marked the start of the serious sports car challenge from the Land of the Rising Sun.

2000 Sports began to make waves at the SCCA races of the day, and owners of traditional sports cars began to take notice. This attention turned into a ground swell of sales when the 2000 Sports evolved into the 240Z. Datsun was not the only Japanese manufacturer with an eye on the sports car market, although in the early days it was the most successful.

It has been said that the spirit of the early British sports cars is clearly linked to the "wind-in-your-face" attitude of the English motor cycle. In fact, many British sports cars, particularly cars such as the Lotus 7, have been called four-wheeled expressions of motor cycles.

ABOVE: The styling of the NSX is reminiscent of many of today's mid-engined supercars, particularly the Ferrari 348, but retains its own identity.

RIGHT: Vents in the door panels pivot up and to the side to help direct air around the NSX cockpit.

If that is the case, then the development of Honda's first sports cars is very significant. Honda in the 1960s came to dominate the world's lightweight motor cycle market, so it was only natural that they carried some of that experience over to their first sports car, the 1962 S500, a 531cc four-cylinder roadster similar to the Austin-Healey Sprites of the day. That car was to evolve into the S600 and S800 – with 606cc and 800cc engines respectively – and eventually more than 12,500 S800s were built. However, none of these cars was officially imported into the United States, and Honda decided to make its US debut with small, economical and reliable sedans.

However, an indication of how seriously Honda took the development of a sporting reputation was the fact that it began development of a Formula One racer in 1962 and took its first F1 victory in 1965 at the Mexico Grand Prix. Today, Honda dominates Formula One, and it has introduced a supercar – the Acura NSX – that can rival the best exotic cars of Europe.

The main contender as the first Japanese sports car that can legitimately claim supercar status is the Toyota 2000GT, which made its debut at the Tokyo Auto Show in October 1965. Designed by the German Albrecht Goertz – who also sculpted the BMW 507 roadster – the 2000GT coupé took the Jaguar XKE head on, in both form and function. The twin-cam, two-litre 150 horsepower, six-cylinder boasted triple side-draught carburettors, tubular manifold and a 7000rpm redline. It was linked to a close-ratio five-speed gearbox, and its top speed was 135mph (217kmh).

A few versions were prepared for SCCA racing in America by Carroll Shelby of Cobra fame, and the top speed of those 200-horsepower cars was more than 150mph (241kmh). Two convertible versions were made for the James Bond film, *You Only Live Twice*, which was set in Japan.

First sold in 1967, the 2000GT was an exotic car in price as well. An American buyer had to pay more than $6,800 to get a 2000GT – above what a comparable XKE would have cost. Toyota records show that only 337 buyers world-wide snapped up the 2000GT during its short production run, and today the Toyota coupé is a much sought-after collectible.

LEFT: The 2000GT was exported to America and Europe, but production numbers were low and the car is now so rare that good examples can cost upward of $100,000 (£56,000).

BELOW: Toyota's 2000GT was the first true exotic car to come out of Japan. A true 135-mph (217-kmh) sports coupé, the 2000GT was virtually hand-built.

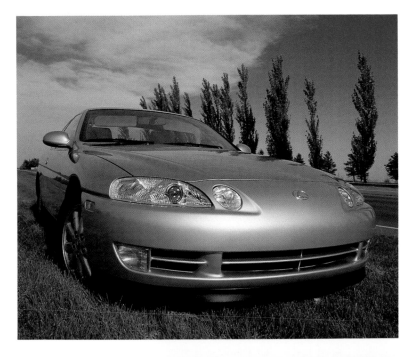

As stylish and exotic as the 2000GT was, Toyota basically abandoned the concept in favour of more mass-produced "sporty" cars such as the Celica. The new Lexus SC400 is the first car since the 2000GT that can even come close to claiming supercar status for Toyota.

Mazda had no such trouble keeping its corporate eye on its goal for a world-class sports car. The Hiroshima-based manufacturer was one of the first companies to take an intense interest in the revolutionary rotary engine developed by Felix Wankel.

The rotary was the basis for Mazda's first legitimate sports car, the Cosmos 110S, which made its debut at the 1964 Tokyo Auto Show and was put into production in 1967. The small, 982cc rotary-engined coupé bears a strong resemblance to a Ferrari Super America, although there

ABOVE: Turning lamps are integrated into the lower edges of the nose on the SC400.

RIGHT: Mazda's 1967 Cosmos was one of the first Japanese supercars.

ABOVE: A Mazda Wankel rotary engine that has been modified by Racing Beat.

BELOW: Mazda's first-generation RX-7 was an instant hit when it made its debut in 1978, and today remains the world's only rotary engined sports car.

addition to the potent engine, the Cosmos also had a true sports car suspension that used twin A-arms up front and a de Dion independent rear axle. Like the 2000GT, few Mazda Cosmos left Japan, and total production was less than 1,100 when it was phased out in 1970. But the Cosmos was the inspiration for the rotary-engined RX-7 that appeared in 1978 and continues to be a significant sports car in the 1990s.

Taken as a whole, the fledgling crop of sports cars that Japan sent into the world nearly three decades ago is hardly impressive. Until the arrival of the 240Z, total production from 1960 to 1970 hardly equalled a single year's production of MGs. Yet these cars set the stage for the great Japanese sports cars of the 1990s – the Mazda RX-7 and Miata; the Nissan 300ZX; the Lexus SC400; the Mitsubishi 3000GT VR-4; and the amazing Acura NSX.

Critics who contend that Japanese sports cars are simply derivations of European models are refusing to look at the facts. By all measures of performance, styling, innovation and price, the sports cars from Japan are setting the pace that other sports car manufacturers around the world are going to have to follow.

are too many afterthoughts among its body features for it to be a really classic design. What was stunning about the car was that Mazda was able to coax 110 horsepower from the two-rotor Wankel engine, which used far fewer parts than a comparable four-cylinder pushrod engine. In

ACURA NSX

TOP SPEED: 168mph (270kmh)

ACCELERATION: 0 to 60mph in 5.2 seconds

ENGINE: Three-litre, 24-valve DOHC V-6

HORSEPOWER: 270bhp @ 7100rpm

If you think only the Italians can make an exotic sports car, you had better steer clear of the Acura NSX. Its alluring shape and the intoxicating sound of its lusty Formula One-bred engine will captivate you, while its impeccable manners will make it your best friend.

HONDA ACURA NSX ツカー

日本のスポーツカー

ABOVE: Acura's NSX is the first true supercar to be built by a Japanese manufacturer. It combines civility with an aggressive design.

Lamborghini, Ferrari, Lotus – they are cars that make your blood rush and your heart ache with desire. Just a photograph of one can make just about any car fanatic lapse into a trance of adoration. These exotic cars are at the leading edge of style and performance. They are extremely fast; they go around corners like a racing car; and they can stop traffic with their aggressive looks. Everyone wants one, but only a few can afford one.

It is perhaps something of a blessing that most people cannot afford these cars, because most drivers would find that the cars of their dreams are far from perfect. They are often difficult to start when cold; they cough and splutter when stuck in hot traffic jams; they have uncomfortable cockpits, the outward visibility of a submarine and the overall mechanical reliability of a Trabant. As one Ferrari acolyte once put it, "These cars are lusty, vibrant automotive statements. If you want an appliance, buy a Japanese car".

What was meant as an insult has come to be a serious – and superior – option in the Acura NSX. In creating the first legitimate Japanese contender to the European supercars, Honda has given birth to a car with all of the attributes of a Ferrari and none of the vices. As usual, that was the goal from the start.

Honda's founder, Soichiro Honda, has always viewed racing and high-performance products as an integral part of the company's operation. When Honda's motor cycles were redefining two-wheeled transportation in the 1960s, Honda was devoting huge resources to winning motor cycle championships. Even before the Honda car was known worldwide, Honda was a viable competitor on the Formula One circuit, scoring its first win in 1965. Now, the Honda-powered McLarens are at the cutting edge of Formula One technology, dominating a sport once the exclusive domain of British and Italian teams.

It was only logical, therefore, that Honda would eventually extend what it had learned on the race track to building the ultimate sports car. The project that would become the Acura NSX began in 1984 at the Tochigi Research and Development Center. The engineers were charged with creating a hand-built, exotic mid-engined sports car that would redefine the genre and be the flagship for the new up-market Acura division.

In keeping with the Japanese practice of studying the opposition intensely, Honda planners looked at limited-production cars such as the Lamborghini Countach, the Ferrari Boxer, Testarossa and 308, the Lotus Esprit and the Porsche 911 Turbo. They looked at mid-range cars such as the Chevrolet Corvette and the Nissan 300ZX. They also looked at the Toyota MR2 and, late in the day, Mazda's MX-5 Miata.

Out of all those comparisons, Honda came up with a target for the ultimate exotic car – it must have exciting styling, amazing power, racing-car handling, yet also be comfortable, have a ride that isn't punishing on city streets, and be as reliable and easy to live with as even the most basic Honda.

There are those who would say – have said, in fact – that all of those goals cannot be accomplished in a single car. Honda said that the phrase "it can't be done" would not be uttered with regard to the NSX. They set their sights high, identifying an American military jet fighter, the General Dynamics F-16 Falcon, as the vehicle that epitomized what they were trying to do. The F-16 had established a reputation among sports-car enthusiasts of being a fast, highly manoeuvrable dogfighter that was lighter and more reliable than its counterparts.

The top priority for the NSX involved weight. Engineers set a target of achieving a power-to-weight ratio of between 11.0 and 12.1lb (4.99 and 5.49kg) per horsepower. To get there, they would have to build a car that weighed about 3,000lb (1,362kg) and had an engine that produced at least 250 horsepower.

To meet the weight goal, aluminium was the only material that was viable, and Honda used it just about everywhere on the NSX – including the frames for the cockpit seats. But aluminium has some serious drawbacks for a road car. Although it is one-third the weight of steel, aluminium is less rigid and therefore more difficult to bend and work into form properly. Since a mid-engined car demands a rigid monocoque chassis, Honda had some considerable hurdles to get over.

To clear those hurdles, engineers reprogrammed Honda's Cray supercomputer to do stress analysis on a theoretical chassis made of aluminium alloys. Working with the characteristics of eight aluminium alloys, the supercomputer helped engineers put together a jigsaw puzzle of varying compositions that eventually became the structure of the NSX.

The end result was a monocoque shell that is significantly stiffer than any other exotic car and, with doors, bonnet and boot lid attached, weighs just 462lb (209.75kg) – 40 per cent less than if it were made of steel.

Because of the rigidity of the monocoque, weight could be saved in setting up the suspension, since the front and rear subframes would not have to bolster the chassis. That allowed Honda to use aluminium alloys extensively to create elegant-looking suspension links that appear spidery, but do the job well.

When it came to using aluminium for the body panels, Honda was unsatisfied with the surface finish on cast alloy panels. They tended to have a slightly rough finish that would not allow the kind of rich paint finish Honda wanted for the NSX. That problem was solved by hand-polishing the dies used to cast the body panels at the new 200-worker plant where the NSX is built.

Overall, the only significant pieces of steel in the NSX chassis and body are a tubular hoop that runs under the dashboard – to support the steering column – and the front and rear bumpers.

With the weight problem solved, Honda set about infusing the NSX with some of the technology it had learned in racing. On the suspension, Honda used a configuration that is similar to the set-up on its Formula One cars. The NSX uses a double wishbone design, with coil springs and anti-sway bars. At the rear, an additional lateral link is used for better wheel control.

BELOW: At a price of about $65,000 (£38,235), the NSX maintains the Japanese hallmark of providing a superior car at an unusually low price.

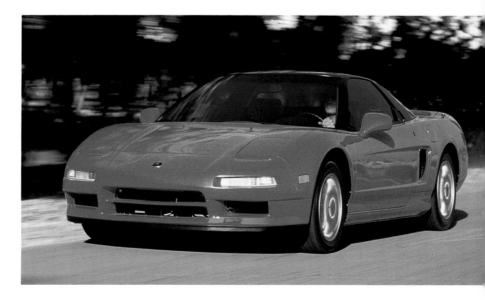

Shock absorbers are gas filled and have been modified with a special piston and valve that vary the damping. Instead of the valve being either open or closed, it opens and closes progressively according to road demands.

To tune the suspension so it would provide superior handling characteristics as well as good everyday performance, Honda tested early NSX prototypes at its Tochigi Proving Grounds, Japan's Suzuka race circuit and Germany's Nurburgring, with world driving champion Ayrton Senna and Indianapolis 500 winner Bobby Rahal behind the wheel.

Avoiding such complex devices as four-wheel steering and computer-controlled shock absorbers, Honda was able to craft a front suspension that uses a compliance pivot strut to reduce toe-in changes, while allowing for wheel camber changes under cornering and reducing the transmission of harsh sensations to the cockpit.

The rear suspension was also modified to improve road handling, with changes in upper and lower control arm bushings, and a shift in the overall suspension geometry to allow limited changes in toe-in under braking, acceleration, and cornering.

Steering on the NSX is a variable ratio rack-and-pinion arrangement, with no power-assist on cars equipped with a manual gearbox. On cars with an automatic gearbox, the steering has a unique electric power-assist system that doesn't draw any power off the engine.

RIGHT: The underside of the rear body panel is sculpted to help air flow under the NSX, much like on a Formula One race car.

Brakes are 11.1in (28.19cm) vacuum-assisted discs all the way around, using steel, rather than aluminium, callipers. Although the steel callipers are heavier, aluminium parts would have been too large for the wheels Honda wanted to use, and the alloy parts showed some wear and tear with hard use.

An anti-lock system is used on the NSX, but it is an upgraded four-channel system that monitors each wheel independently using a 16-bit microprocessor. That allows better control if the car is under hard braking and one side is on a wet or oily surface and the other is on a dry surface.

The tyres on the NSX are similarly well tuned. Working with the Yokohama Rubber Company, Honda entered into a two-year search for optimum performance tyres. More than 100 versions were tried before tyres for the NSX were chosen. In the end, the size and rubber compound of the front and rear tyres were staggered for a variety of reasons.

At the front, the NSX has 205/50ZR-15 tyres that have a slightly different tread pattern and are about 10 per cent softer than the rear tyres. At the back, Honda uses 225/50ZR-16 tyres. The NSX has forged aluminium alloy wheels that are 6.5in (16.5cm) wide for the front and 8in (20.32cm) wide for the rear. In keeping with the weight-saving philosophy of the NSX, the forged wheels are about 13lb (5.9kg) lighter than cast aluminium versions.

Not only did the staggering of the tyre sizes and using lightweight wheels allow Honda to fine-tune the NSX's handling, the smaller tyres at the front meant that the footwells in the interior could be more spacious.

To go with such a world-class chassis, Honda had to come up with a world-class engine. The engine compartment is the heart of any exotic sports car, not only for the power it provides, but also the soul-stirring sounds that come from a high-revving engine.

With its Formula One experience as a benchmark, Honda engineers looked for an engine that met several key goals. It had to be lightweight, produce more than 250 horsepower, generate lots of low-end torque, but also create high-end power, and be as tractable and reliable as a basic Honda.

Early on, engineers decided that an aluminium block V-6 was a good basic engine. They examined the option of adding turbochargers or superchargers, but dismissed those because of poor throttle response and a feeling that such additions were too complex for the car they were building. So they started with a normally aspirated three-litre, 90-degree V-6, and used a variety of new technologies to increase its output to supercar levels.

Inside the aluminium block, Honda installed a counterweighted, forged steel crankshaft, superlight titanium alloy connecting rods from the Formula One engines, and special aluminium alloy pistons. The use of the titanium connecting

LEFT: Special forged alloy wheels helped save critical weight on the NSX.

BELOW: Honda engineers have managed to get 270 horsepower from the NSX engine by using several very unusual modifications.

rods – the first such application in a street car – greatly reduced internal power loss and helped the engine achieve high rpms with less effort.

Topping the aluminium block are double overhead camshaft cylinder heads, made from a different aluminium alloy, that are designed to resist stress cracks and improve combustion. Each of the chambers has four valves and a platinum-tipped spark plug that is fired by its own individual coil, thus eliminating the need for a standard distributor.

As complicated as all of this may sound, the real key to the power Honda managed to unlock from its V-6 is an extremely advanced camshaft/valve actuating system called VTEC – Variable Valve Timing and Lift Electronic Control System. The point of the VTEC system is to provide low-end torque and high-end power with none of the usual drawbacks.

On each cylinder in a normal four-valve double overhead camshaft engine, there are two camshaft lobes that operate the intake valves, and two that work the exhaust valves. Throughout the rpm range of the engine, the valves open and close in exactly the same way, whether the engine is turning at 2,000rpm or 6,000rpm. So the camshaft lobes that open the valves are shaped in such a way as to compromise low-rpm power with high-rpm efficiency.

In traditional exotic cars, such as the Ferrari, the camshafts are tuned to provide most of the power at high rpms, so in low-speed conditions those engines are less efficient and more balky.

Honda found the best of both worlds by adding a third lobe to the camshaft for each cylinder. At low engine speeds, the added lobe is not engaged and the two main lobes act in a manner that opens and closes the valves to enhance torque and power up to 5,800rpm. Above that speed, a computer sends a signal that engages the third camshaft lobe, which forces the valves to open and close in a different manner better suited to producing power in high-rpm conditions. Honda says that the VTEC feature engages in less than a tenth of a second and adds about 20 horsepower to the NSX engine.

Another method that blends torque and horsepower is a system that Honda calls Variable Volume Induction. This set-up uses a second magnesium plenum that is mounted beneath the main induction manifold and the two are linked by six vacuum-activated butterfly valves. Up to 4,800rpm, air runs into the main intake manifold, which feeds it separately to the front and rear cylinders, creating a resonance effect that enhances low- and mid-range torque. Above 4,800rpm, the butterfly valves open, creating one large chamber that feeds all six cylinders. The

LEFT: The indicator and parking lights are recessed into the front bumper and fender assembly.

Power is fed to the rear wheels through either a five-speed manual gearbox or a four-speed automatic gearbox. The manual gearbox uses a twin-disc clutch that needs significantly less pedal pressure to operate than in many exotic cars.

Offering an automatic gearbox in an exotic car is almost heresy to some fans of supercars, but it is right in line with Honda's thinking that the NSX should be a car that can be comfortable in all conditions. With the automatic, the NSX engine is retuned for additional torque, so horsepower drops to 252.

A last little refinement that Honda added to the NSX was the Traction Control System. Although traction control has been around for several years, the NSX unit is among the smarter systems. Using the speed sensors that are a part of the anti-lock braking system – and other sensors that monitor speed and steering angle – the NSX system determines whether the rear wheels are spinning because of icy or wet conditions, acceleration or high-speed cornering and adjusts engine speed accordingly. The car starts with the system on, but the driver can turn it off by pushing a button on the dashboard.

LEFT: The engine is separated from the cockpit by a glass panel, then is covered by a carpeted panel and a lift-up glass hatch.

resonance effect is reduced, but a ram air effect is created that improves the engine's breathing at high rpms and increases horsepower.

Add to these unique high-tech improvements such routine features as programmed fuel injection and a 10.2 to 1 compression ratio, and the NSX V-6 produces 270 horsepower at 7,100rpm.

The engine is mounted transversely behind the passenger cockpit, covered by a carpeted panel and enclosed by a glass hatch cover.

BELOW: The use of pop-up headlights allowed designers to keep the bonnet line low.

With such a formidable chassis and drive line combination to move the NSX along, Honda stylists wanted a shape that would tell the world the NSX was a true supercar. Again, the influence of the F-16 fighter jet and the Formula One racing cars would have a profound impact. Because of the transverse positioning of the engine in a central location, the NSX shares some of the basic design cues of such cars as the Ferrari 348, namely a wide stance, a long tail and a short nose.

However, the Honda designers managed to give the NSX a look of its own by seeking to enhance the driving experience through the placement of the cockpit. Honda says it set out to duplicate two experiences – that of a racing car driver and a jet fighter pilot. The racing driver, they reasoned, needs to be positioned at the nose of the car so he can see everything that is happening at 200mph (320kmh); so too does the fighter pilot need to feel as though he is actually out in the windstream.

As a result, a canopy effect was created for the NSX, and the cockpit is almost a bubble that is positioned far forwards in the body. To enhance that look even further, the canopy body panels are painted black to attract the eye to that part of the car.

In front of the cockpit is a short, wide, sloping nose that uses pop-up headlights to increase the front rake. A small, split mouth is the main feature of the plastic front end cap, which features recessed parking lights and indicators, and a chin spoiler.

Back from the cockpit is a long tail that ends in a plastic rear bumper assemby that, viewed from the back, looks like the underbody air tunnels seen on Formula One cars. An integral spoiler tops the rear, which opens up to allow access to a serviceable boot.

On the side panels are two large air intake ducts that feed the engine. The one on the left side sends air to the engine's combustion chamber, the one on the right – along with the front scoop – feeds the radiator.

An interesting note about Honda's obsession with perfection concerns the duct that feeds fresh air to the engine. It seems that the rush of air created a booming sound that could be heard in the cockpit, so engineers altered the plumbing to avert the offending noise.

Overall, the NSX is a relatively large car. It is 174.3in (442.7cm) long, with a wheelbase of 99.6in (252.9cm), a width of 71.3in (181.1cm) and a height of 46.1in (117.1cm). With its short nose, bubble cockpit and long tail, the NSX bears

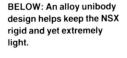

BELOW: An alloy unibody design helps keep the NSX rigid and yet extremely light.

SPECIFICATIONS

DIMENSIONS

Wheelbase: 99.6in (253.0cm)
Overall length: 173.4in (440.4cm)
Width: 71.3in (181.1cm)
Height: 46.1in (117.1cm)
Front Track: 59.4in (150.9cm)
Rear Track: 60.2in (152.9cm)
Weight: 3,010lb (1,366.5kg)
Fuel capacity: 18.5gall (70.0l)

ENGINE

24-valve, DOHC V-6
Aluminium block and cylinder heads
Programmed electronic fuel injection
Bore and Stroke: 3.64 × 3.07in (8.99 × 7.80cm)
Displacement: 2977cc
Compression Ratio: 10.2:1
Horsepower: Net 270bhp @ 7100rpm
Torque: Net 210lb-ft @ 5300rpm
Redline: 8000rpm

GEARBOX

Five-speed manual overdrive
Gear ratios: (1) 3.07 (2) 1.73 (3) 1.23 (4) 0.97
(5) 0.77
Rear end ratio: 4.06:1

SUSPENSION

Four-wheel independent
Upper and lower A-arms with pivot point strut at front
Upper and lower A-arms with trailing link at back
Coil springs
Front and rear anti-roll bars

STEERING

Rack and pinion, variable ratio
Turns, lock-to-lock: 3.2
Turning circle: 38.2ft (11.6m)

BRAKES

Power-assisted four-wheel discs with anti-lock
Disc size: 11.1in (28.2cm) front, 11.1in (28.2cm) rear

WHEELS AND TYRES

Forged aluminium wheels, 15 × 6.5in (38.1 × 6.5cm) front, 16 × 8in (40.6 × 20.3cm) rear
Yokohama A-022, 205/50ZR-15 front, 225/50ZR-16 rear

a resemblance to the Porsche 917 racing cars of the 1970s and early 1980s.

Inside the NSX, Honda worked especially hard at making a supercar that is extremely friendly. Some of the drawbacks that Honda found on most mid-engined exotic cars were that the cockpit was cramped, the controls were poorly placed, visibility was restricted and climate control was weak.

Because of the forward-cockpit design, the NSX rewards the driver with great front visibility. Large side windows and a wide rear window eliminate most blind spots, and the power side mirrors also provide good rear visibility.

The leather-covered, electrically adjustable seats can be moved a considerable distance fore and aft to accommodate just about any driver. The steering wheel, with an air-bag supplementary restraint system, is adjustable for reach and rake.

ABOVE: Fresh air is fed to the engine from this duct on the driver's side of the NSX.

RIGHT: The automatic gear stick resides in the centre console. An automatic gearbox is an unusual offering in an exotic car.

Honda resisted the temptation to use gimmicks on the instrument panel, opting instead for clear, white-on-black gauges with red needles. A 185mph (297kmh) speedometer and an 8,500rpm tachometer are in the centre of the instrument pod and are flanked by four gauges for oil pressure, voltage, engine temperature and fuel level.

A high centre console contains a storage bin, the parking brake, gear stick, cigarette lighter, radio and stereo cassette player, and controls and vents for the automatic temperature system. On the doors are controls for the power windows, door locks and two adjustable vents for cockpit airflow. Also, in front of the passenger is a large storage bin.

The NSX interior is a direct descendant of the cockpit found in the Acura Legend Coupé, one of the most comfortable luxury cars on the road.

ABOVE: Ample air vents and strong air-conditioner enhance the NSX cockpit cooling system.

RIGHT: An upswept rear design and a full-width spoiler give the NSX a very racy appeal.

To wrap up this impressive package of style, engineering, power and comfort, Honda has added its standard three-year, 36,000 mile (58,000km) warranty, an indication that it is confident the NSX will be as reliable as its Civic saloons have been.

Such a car was bound to have instant appeal, particularly when Honda priced it at $62,000 (£36,470) – nearly $40,000 (£23,529) under a comparable Ferrari and less than half the price of a Lamborghini. When the NSX made its debut in 1990, dealers were swamped with orders and some customers paid as much as $30,000 (£17,650) over the manufacturer's price to secure one. Thankfully, such buyer mania has died down and the NSX has been able to take its place as a bargain-priced exotic car that can do everything better than most traditional supercars.

DRIVING IMPRESSIONS

The stretch of road was the famous Mulholland Drive in the hills above Los Angeles. It was a quiet afternoon and the road that winds among secluded multimillion-dollar homes was virtually empty.

The red Acura NSX was running along at a speed that would gain the driver a speeding ticket should any police car happen to spot it. But I was not concerned because I was at one with the machine on this warm sunny day, and all was right with the world.

On the straight stretches, the V-6 howled at a fevered pitch, throwing off delicious noises just behind my back. When a curve came up, the NSX turned into it with great aplomb, rounded the bend at speed without any alarming twitches and then straightened up for the next burst of speed, the engine urging me to seek its 8,000rpm ceiling.

When the volume of traffic dictated a much slower pace, the NSX became docile. The engine ticked over quietly, the gauges all stayed at normal levels, and the NSX behaved impeccably. When the road was clear, the Acura was all snarls and speed at a moment's notice.

Makers of Ferraris, Lotuses and Lamborghinis should hang their heads in shame when an NSX passes by. Honda has created a car with all of the excitement of a European exotic car and none of the vices.

On the performance side, the NSX runs to 60mph (96.5kmh) in 5.2 seconds, speeds through the quarter-mile (0.4km) in 13.7 seconds and has a top speed of 168mph (270kmh). It stops forcefully, handles like an open-wheeled racing car and has such good manners it can make just about anyone look like Michael Andretti.

Steering runs to mild understeer and it is just about impossible to make the rear end twitchy, unlike most mid-engined exotic cars. Power is there on demand at any point in the rev band.

And there are no trade offs for all of this. Creeping along in bumper-to-bumper traffic, the NSX could be a Honda Civic for all the problems it shows. Stuck in a traffic jam on a 90-degree day in Los Angeles, the temperature gauge never made a move towards the danger zone.

The interior of the NSX is as comfortable as any car on the road. The seats are very supportive without feeling like strait-jackets, and they adjust through a wide range of settings, as does the steering wheel. The air-conditioning works without complaint, the controls for lights, cruise control, indicators and radio are clearly marked and within easy reach. The fit and finish were excellent – even with 20,000 miles (32,000km) showing on the odometer.

The styling is as aggressive as any supercar, and in car-jaded Los Angeles the NSX attracted the attention that should come with any sports car that costs more than $60,000 (£35,000).

About the only complaint I have is that the NSX doesn't come with a lift-out roof panel. You see, I just couldn't get enough of the intoxicating sounds coming from that wonderful V-6.

LEXUS SC 400

TOP SPEED: 150mph (241kmh)

ACCELERATION: 0 to 60mph in 6.5 seconds

ENGINE: Four-litre, 32-valve DOHC V-8

HORSEPOWER: 250bhp @ 5600rpm

Who says a high-performance luxury coupé has to be bland and boring? Not Toyota, who created the extraordinary shape of the Lexus SC400 by massaging clay-filled balloons, bringing that shell to life with a V-8 heart.

日本のLEXUS SC400ポーツカー

Lexus SC400: A World-class Coupé Debut

日本のスポーツカー

RIGHT: To retain the very rounded shape of the nose, Toyota engineers split the main beam and high-beam headlights, creating a very appealing styling edge.

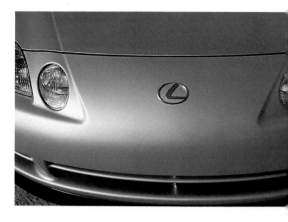

In 1990, Japanese car giant Toyota redefined the luxury sports saloon when it introduced its Lexus LS400 saloon in the United States. Part of an upscale marketing move begun nearly five years earlier by Honda with its Acura division, the Lexus went even further. For a fully optioned price of about $40,000 (£23,529), the LS 400 saloon offered a four-litre, 32-valve V-8 that produced 250 very smooth horsepower, a soft yet capable suspension, and a list of amenities to rival any saloon on the road.

The arrival of the Lexus sent ripples through the luxury market that had come to be dominated by BMW, Mercedes and Jaguar – these manufacturers found their cars now faced a competitor priced thousands, if not tens of thousands, below their comparable vehicles.

As impressive as the Lexus saloon was when it made its debut, it gave just a hint of the flagship luxury sports car Lexus brought to the market in June 1991. Called the SC400, the new Lexus coupé is one of the most stylish, refined and aggressive cars in the world today. There are those who might argue that it isn't a true sports car, but the facts say otherwise.

A car that can top 150mph (241.35kmh), generate nearly eight-tenths of a G in lateral adhesion,

BELOW: Inlets below the SC400's nose allow sufficient air into the engine compartment to cool the V-8 engine.

hit 60mph (96.54kmh) in 6.5 seconds and do it all without rattling the driver, definitely qualifies as a supercar by most objective standards.

But even though the Lexus stands out on its performance alone, the styling of the coupé will make it one of the all-time great car shapes, particularly in an era when most production cars have very run-of-the-mill shapes. The SC400 owes its styling to a dedicated group of designers at Toyota's US styling studio – Calty Design Research in Newport Beach, California – and the conviction of Seihachi Takahashi, the coupé's chief engineer in Japan.

In Toyota's product tree, the SC400 is the blossom that replaces the Soarer, Toyota's flagship coupé in Japan. But when work began in 1987 on the Soarer replacement, Toyota knew that the new car also would be the star of its soon-to-be-born Lexus division in the United States.

So it became an uncompromising goal that the new coupé would have a look that would cause heads to turn, particularly in car-crazy Southern California. To meet that goal, design teams at Calty and at Toyota in Japan were put into head-to-head competition to create the most innovative new design.

Calty designer Erwin Lui, working under the direction of Dennis Campbell, senior chief designer, took a very tactile approach to creating the shape of the SC400. Called "touch sculpture", Lui poured clay into latex balloons and spent hundreds of hours massaging the mass. And it was a painstaking task, because Lui used potters' clay instead of the normal industrial clay and the potters' clay took more effort to mould – effort Lui hoped would show in the final shape.

Settling at last on a shape that Lui called "an elongated bow tie", the Calty staff began turning the clay-filled balloon into something that would ride on four wheels. Their first effort was not practical enough for the real world, so it was discarded in favour of a model that was more workable, but still had a few too many show-car touches, such as a clamshell bonnet, similar to the Corvette.

Still, the design was close enough that Calty began the process of lobbying the decision-makers back in Japan to accept their design in principle. They were up against a home office design that sacrificed elegance for a futuristic "Terminator" look.

With some relatively minor changes – the clamshell bonnet was axed – the Calty design carried the day. But as any designer knows, it's a long

BELOW: Toyota designers in the United States used innovative methods, such as hand-kneeding clay-filled balloons, to come up with the SC400's shape.

way from drawing board to assembly line, and the SC400's shape provided quite a few manufacturing challenges. For example, the graceful yet powerful front nose was so rounded that many traditional mounting points for such things as headlights and a battery were very tight, and ventilation for the V-8 engine was in doubt.

But the SC400's shape had won over chief engineer Takahashi, who decreed that solutions would be found to these and other problems. To take care of the headlight problem, the high-beams were split off from the main beams and sculpted into the nose. The cooling problem was solved through the use of an electronically controlled hydraulic fan system, which moves more air through the radiator and reduces noise and engine load. And the boot opening was enlarged slightly to make it easier to fit the car's petrol tank on the assembly line.

BELOW: Viewed from the top, the curvaceous nature of the Lexus coupé shows through clearly. There is not a single straight line in the SC400's design.

Another difficult point overcome by sharp engineering was access to the SC400's small but serviceable back seat. Originally, Calty's design called for small "service hatch" doors to get to the two rear seats; but that was quickly discarded as being too avant-garde. Instead, Toyota engineers redesigned the hinge that holds the massive doors. A four-link hinge allows the door to move forwards and to tilt outwards at the top when it is opened. Also, the front seat automatically moves forwards when the seat back is released, then returns to its original position when the seat back is upright again.

All in all, the SC400's coachwork survived the to-and-fro of the manufacturing process remarkably intact. But if the SC400 had been just another pretty face, it hardly would have qualified for supercar status. At the root of the SC400's performance charm is the 3,969 cubic centimetre V-8 that is lifted mostly intact from the LS400 saloon. It is an all-aluminium creation that has four valves per cylinder, actuated by two overhead camshafts.

Fuel is delivered through a multiport electronic injection system, which is monitored by an anti-knock sensor that keeps the engine from developing a knock under acceleration. For maximum performance from the 250-horsepower engine, premium unleaded fuel is required. Although the SC400 will make do with ordinary unleaded, it will deliver fewer horsepower.

Although redline for the free-breathing V-8 is 6,500rpm, the Lexus churns out its horsepower and torque considerably below that level. Peak horsepower is at 5,600rpm, and the engine's maximum of 260 foot-pounds of torque is reached at 4,400rpm.

To date, the only gearbox available in the SC400 is a four-speed electronically controlled automatic. Although the absence of a five-, or six-speed manual is a serious oversight, the overdrive automatic is a competent piece of machinery.

As an enhancement to fuel economy, the gearbox will normally start in second gear unless a heavy foot on the accelerator demands first gear. Gear changes are made smoother than normal because the gear box computer calculates gear points and then subtly alters engine speed to ensure an almost unnoticeable gear change. The

ABOVE: An all-aluminium engine, the SC400's four-litre V-8 is the same engine that comes in the larger Lexus LS400 saloon. It propels the coupé to a rev-limited maximum speed of 155mph (249.40kmh).

RIGHT: A very comfortable interior marks the SC400's cockpit, thanks in part to an electrically operated tilt steering wheel.

transmission of power to the rear wheels is further ironed out by the use of a special "high-perform-ance" fluid and a "super flow" torque converter.

An option that most SC400s sold in cold-weather climates get is traction control, a black-box computer system that monitors rear wheel spin and retards the engine and applies the rear brakes whenever the tyres start to slip. For those who like to light up the tyres, however, the system can be turned on and off by the touch of a button on the centre console in the cockpit.

Although the SC400 coupé shares many of its chassis components with its saloon sibling, im-portant changes were made to make sure that the coupé behaves more like a sports car than a town car. Starting with a wheelbase that is nearly 5in (12.7cm) shorter than the LS400 saloon, engineers began playing with the double-wish-bone set-up that controls the movement at each of the four wheels.

Using lightweight aluminium parts, the SC400's upper front suspension arms are linked down low to a subframe assembly, rather than the body, for increased lateral rigidity and better handling. The lower control arms were made more compliant for forward and backward motions, and a small kingpin was added to im-prove control under heavy braking.

At the back, the gas-charged shock absorbers are attached to the lower wishbone arms and the upper wishbone arms are mounted lower, creat-ing a suspension that is both more rigid yet less prone to transmitting road noises to the interior.

SPECIFICATIONS

DIMENSIONS

Wheelbase: 105.9in (268.99cm)
Overall length: 191.1in (485.39cm)
Width: 70.5in (179.07cm)
Height: 52.6in (133.60cm)
Front Track: 59.8in (151.89cm)
Rear Track: 60.0in (152.40cm)
Weight: 3,575lb (1,623.05kg)
Fuel capacity: 20.6gall (77.98l)

ENGINE

32-valve, DOHC V-8
Aluminium block and heads
Multipoint electronic fuel injection
Bore and Stroke: 3.44 × 3.25in (8.74 × 8.26cm)
Displacement: 3969cc
Compression Ratio: 10.0:1
Horsepower: Net 250bhp @ 5600rpm
Torque: Net 260lb-ft @ 4400rpm
Redline: 6500rpm

GEARBOX

Four-speed overdrive automatic
Gear ratios: (1) 2.80 (2) 1.53 (3) 1.00 (4) 0.71
Rear end ratio: 3.92:1

SUSPENSION

Four-wheel independent
Upper and lower A-arms
Coil springs
Front and rear anti-roll bars

STEERING

Rack and pinion
Variable ratio, power-assisted
Turns, lock-to-lock: 3.1
Turning circle: 36.1ft (11.00m)

BRAKES

Power-assisted four-wheel discs
Disc size: 11.7in (29.72cm) front, 12.1in (30.73cm) rear
Computer-controlled anti-lock system

WHEELS AND TYRES

16 × 7in (40×15.5cm) cast aluminium wheels
225/55VR-16 Goodyear Eagle GSD radials

Brakes are also changed. The front discs are 11.7in (29.72cm), with the rear discs measuring 12.1in (30.73cm). The four-wheel-disc system is vacuum assisted and connected to a computer-controlled anti-lock system.

Wheels are 10-spoke, 16in (40.64cm) alloys that are 7in (17.78cm) wide. Mounted to all US models are 225/55 VR-16 Goodyear Eagle GSD radials. Less aggressive than the all-out Goodyear Eagle "Gatorback" performance tyres, the GSD rubber is a compromise design that offers considerable grip yet is more compliant over rough roads.

In between the body and the frame, the SC400 uses lots of asphalt sheeting, foam rubber and felt, as well as high tensile steel and other chassis and cabin reinforcements to make the coupé a tight, vibration-free vehicle.

The aim of making the cockpit a place of both power and refinement carries over into the interior design of the SC400. Although technically a 2+2 design, the SC400's cockpit is arranged so that two people can be transported at high speeds in some style and comfort. Seats are upholstered in leather, as are the door panels and portions of the dashboard, and wool carpets

cover the floor and the lower kick panels. Bird's eye maple accents run at eye level across the dashboard and the doors. A large centre console, housing the climate control system and the sound system, as well as the gear stick, separates the two front bucket seats.

In front of the driver is a pod of gauges dominated by a large tachometer and speedometer. Two auxiliary gauges – one for fuel, the other for engine temperature – flank the speedometer

ABOVE: A clue to the SC400's sporting nature can be found in the large dual exhaust pipes that run from the V-8 to the back.

LEFT: The Lexus SC400 coupé is one of the most stunning designs of the 1990s.

RIGHT: The wide track of the Lexus gives it handling characteristics on a par with most sports cars.

and the tachometer, and there is a digital clock and odometer, as well as journey mileage counter. Warning lights make up the remainder of the dashboard pod, which is illuminated through a backlit system that makes all the dials very readable both day and night. Controls for the indicators, lights, windscreen washer/wipers and cruise control are found on three stalks sticking out from the steering column.

The steering wheel, which contains an air-bag supplementary restraint system, both tilts and telescopes electrically at the touch of a button on the left side of the steering column. A second button will cause the wheel to swing up to make it easier to get in and out of the cockpit.

Seats are motorized for infinite adjustment, and electrically heated seat bottoms are optional. An additional feature is a standard seat memory system that allows two people to set their favourite seat/steering wheel position and then, upon pressing the appropriate button, recall it should the seat be out of kilter when they slide behind the wheel.

Another bit of technology shows up in the oddest place – the rear-view mirror. Rather than use the conventional method of reducing glare from following headlights at night by adjusting the position of the mirror, Toyota engineers have developed a mirror that uses liquid crystals to darken the mirror at the touch of a button.

Although the SC400 contains many features, the option list is short yet significant. Apart from the traction-control system – a $1,500 option – there is a rear spoiler (a must from a styling point of view), a power tilt-and-slide moonroof and a remote-control Nachamichi compact disc sound system that features a 12-disc changer that is mounted in the boot. Also available is a factory-installed hands-free cellular phone and a remote-controlled security system that makes an SC400 very difficult to steal.

Overall, it is an impressive package of performance, style and refinement that is unavailable at anything near its basic price of $37,500 (£22,060). Fully loaded with options, an SC400 will cost in the region of $44,000 (£25,882) – a bargain when compared with other super coupés from more traditional European manufacturers.

DRIVING IMPRESSIONS

Think of the punch of a prize fighter delivered in a velvet boxing glove: a wallop that is so smooth you hardly feel it. That's the way the SC400 behaves on the road. Slide into the soft leather driver's seat, hear the smooth, high-tech whine as the electric motor moves the steering wheel into position, and then start up the four-litre V-8.

If the SC400's windows are up, you have to glance at the bright lights of the dashboard to make sure the V-8 is running. If the windows are down, you can hear the 32 valves of the V-8 clicking contentedly, along with the slight rumble from the dual exhausts. Put the gear stick into drive and the Lexus moves forward effortlessly

Ask for a little throttle, and the SC400 responds like a cabin cruiser moving away from the dock. Demand a lot of throttle, and the Lexus surges ahead like an offshore racing boat, the burble from the exhaust becoming a muted yet significant roar.

Sensations of speed are deceiving in the SC400, because the car never seems to be moving as fast as it really is. When the speedometer says 80mph (128kmh), the car feels as though it's moving at 50mph (80kmh). Above 80mph (128kmh), the car gives a steady ride and feels utterly stable.

Turn into a curve, and the SC400 reminds you it's a heavy car by exhibiting mild understeer. Yet it's a manageable amount that never becomes obtrusive. In fact, on particularly winding roads it's possible to toss the SC400 from apex to apex with total control. If the back end gets out of line, just ease off the accelerator and the Lexus regains its aplomb.

Overall, the Lexus SC400 is a near-perfect coupé. It has ample power for most situations, and its handling characteristics allow most drivers to play amateur Grand Prix driver without sacrificing comfort.

There are a couple of niggling points: the seats need more side bolstering for when hard driving moves the driver about; and some of the air-conditioning controls are out of reach.

But it seems so minor to complain about anything in a car that performs so well and looks so stunning as the SC400.

MITSUBISHI 3000GT VR-4

TOP SPEED: 155mph (249kmh)

ACCELERATION: 0 to 60mph in 5 seconds

ENGINE: Turbocharged three-litre, 24-valve DOHC V-6

HORSEPOWER: 296bhp @ 5500rpm

The 1990s are the era of automotive high-technology, and the Mitsubishi 3000GT VR-4 is the mascot. Take a provocative shape and stuff it with every bell and whistle, from twin turbos to all-wheel drive, and you've got the 3000GT VR-4 — an instant supercar.

日 MITSUBISHI 3000GT VR-4 カー

日本のスポーツカー

Building a sports car in the 1990s is a lot like playing in a high-stakes card game. Just when you think you've got a winning hand, the person across from you gives an evil grin and raises the stakes by a considerable margin. At that moment, you just know your hand is not going to be good enough.

That is how the world's car makers, particularly those that build high-performance sports cars, must have felt when Mitsubishi unveiled its 3000GT VR-4 in 1991. If that sounds a bit of an exaggeration, try to name another sports car that has a twin-turbo, twin-intercooled V-6 that produces 296 horsepower, full-time all-wheel drive, speed-sensitive four-wheel steering, a computer-controlled suspension, a speed-activated system of aerodynamic aids and an exhaust system that can be tuned for either power or quiet via a switch in the cockpit. It goes from 0 to 60mph (96.5kmh) in about five seconds, has a top speed of about 160mph (257.4kmh) and costs under $35,000.

BELOW: All-wheel drive and four-wheel steering are standard on the VR-4 model.

What Mitsubishi set out to do was to cram every bit of high-tech gadgetry available into its 2 + 2 3000GT, making it one of the most advanced sports cars on the planet.

Despite its credentials, the 3000GT can trace its lineage to a very unimpressive sporty car called the Starion. A rear-wheel-drive car, the Starion was initially conceived as competition for the Nissan Z cars of the 1980s. However, with its boxy styling and modest performance and handling characteristics, the Starion was, by most measures, a failure. So, when Mitsubishi began planning for the car that would become the company's top-of-the-line replacement for the Starion, they literally started with a clean sheet of paper.

However, before the first line was drawn, some basic marketing decisions were made about the new car. Drawing in part on the marketing strategy made famous by General Motors founder Alfred P Sloan, Mitsubishi decided the new car would be offered in multiple stages of tuning and

ABOVE: The 3000GT SL looks almost identical to the VR-4, but there's a big difference in performance and handling.

equipment. This was especially important because Mitsubishi would be sharing the new car with its close US partner, Chrysler. Although the car would be designed and built in Japan, it would also be available at Chrysler's Dodge dealers under the name Stealth. And Chrysler was insistent that a basic-level vehicle should be manufactured and sold for a price of just under $17,000 (£10,000).

While the ultimate goal was to make a no-holds-barred sports car, the initial platform would have to be flexible enough to accommodate a bargain-basement model. The rear-wheel-drive platform that had propelled the Starion was discarded in favour of a front-wheel-drive set-up that could draw from Mitsubishi's other front-wheel-drive cars. The basis for the 3000GT is the chassis used in the Eclipse, a very cheaply priced sports coupé that uses four-cylinders for power

and employs front-wheel-drive in its most common model.

Wheelbase for the 3000GT and the Eclipse are an identical 97.2in (246.88cm), but that is about the only specification the two cars share. The 3000GT is a wide 72.4in (183.90cm), with an overall length of 178.9in (454.41cm).

The car with the least frills – Dodge's Stealth – uses a single overhead camshaft V-6 that is fuel injected and produces 164 horsepower to drive the front wheels. This model is plain to such a degree that Mitsubishi doesn't even offer a comparable version.

At Mitsubishi, the 3000GT range starts with a version that offers a double overhead camshaft, fuel-injected V-6 that produces 222 horsepower. The power is transmitted to the front wheels through either a four-speed automatic or a five-speed manual gearbox.

A step up from the basic 3000GT is the 3000GT SL, which uses the same running gear but offers upgraded equipment that includes a computer-controlled suspension system and an anti-lock system for the four-wheel disc brakes.

Although these cars are impressive, they pale into insignificance when compared to the top model, the 3000GT VR-4. To create the VR-4 model, the engineers at Mitsubishi began by building an engine that uses just about every trick to generate horsepower and still meet the strict US emissions standards.

Each bank of three cylinders in the 60-degree V-6 engine gets its own turbocharger and intercooler. The boost from the Mitsubishi TD04 turbos begins to make itself known just above 1,000rpm and eventually produces maximum boost of 9.7psi at about 5,500rpm. But there's more to the V-6 than a couple of strong lungs. The iron-block engine is topped with special aluminium cylinder heads with pent-roof combustion chambers producing an 8:1 compression ratio. Each cylinder contains four valves and the engine's total 24 valves are activated by four camshafts driven by a single cogged belt. In addition, hydraulic valve-lash adjusters and aluminium rocker arms with needle-bearing rollers help increase horsepower through less friction.

To strengthen the engine, there are forged connecting rods and steel-reinforced aluminium pistons. Fuel is fed to the V-6 through a computer-controlled multipoint injection system. The result is 296 horsepower and 307 foot-pounds of torque.

Once they had turned out such a muscular engine for the 3000GT, Mitsubishi engineers were faced with the task of how to make the most of all that power. Since they began with a platform designed for front-wheel drive, the engineers really had only one choice – adding a drive line to the rear wheels for four-wheel drive.

To move the engine's torque around the chassis, Mitsubishi developed an all-wheel-drive system that, under normal conditions, splits the power so that 45 per cent goes to the front wheels and 55 per cent goes to the rear. Power is moved around by a viscous coupling unit centre differential, which monitors what is happening at both the front and back. When the viscous coupling unit senses one axle is getting less grip, it shifts power to the other axle. In extreme conditions, it can send all the power to either the front or rear wheels.

In part because of the hefty amounts of torque produced by the V-6, Mitsubishi did not have an automatic gearbox that would work with the 3000GT VR-4, so they turned instead to the

LEFT: A marvel of engineering, the VR-4's twin-turbo V-6 produces nearly 100 horsepower per litre.

German company Getrag for a five-speed manual gearbox, which is the only one available in the VR-4 model.

With a sophisticated drivetrain in place, Mitsubishi next went to work on the suspension of the VR-4. At the front, there is a coil-spring arrangement that uses a forward cross-member, lower control arms and an anti-roll bar. At the back is a similar coil-spring arrangement with both upper and lower semi-trailing arms, lower transverse links and an anti-roll bar.

The shock absorbers are also adjustable through what is called an electronically controlled suspension. The system is linked to a switch in the cockpit that allows the driver to select two settings: touring and sport. In the touring mode, a computer monitors the car's speed, cornering and suspension and will automatically switch the shocks to one of three settings – soft, medium and firm – depending on what is needed at the time. In the sport mode, the shock absorbers are kept locked in the firm setting.

To this suspension Mitsubishi added a hydraulically activated four-wheel-steering system. Unlike some four-wheel-steering systems, the one

ABOVE:
Mitsubishi's 3000GT, in the foreground, is a direct descendant of the HSR-II prototype.

RIGHT: A Mitsubishi takes a sharp turn at the Jim Russell School, where high-performance driving techniques are taught.

on the 3000GT is designed strictly to aid high-speed cornering. The system comes alive at speeds above 30mph (48.3kmh). When the steering wheel is turned, a computer monitors the speed of the car, how fast the steering wheel is being turned and the lateral force being exerted on the toe-control member of the rear suspension. Under certain conditions, the system allows the rear wheels to be turned up to 1.5 degrees in the same direction as the front wheels are turned, making cornering manoeuvres sharper.

Stopping power on the VR-4 is considerable, thanks to huge disc brakes at all four wheels. At the front, the brakes are 16in (40.64cm) vented discs, with 15in (38.1cm) units at the back. The callipers are a four-piston design, and the power-assisted brakes are linked to a two-channel anti-lock system.

Rounding off the chassis are cast-alloy 17in (43.18cm) wheels that carry 245/45VR Goodyear "Gatorback" high-performance tyres.

Taken on the technical merits mentioned so far, the Mitsubishi 3000GT VR-4 is a car that has impressive credentials – so impressive that it won *Motor Trend*'s coveted Import Car of the Year award in 1991. But the engineers had two other items they wanted to add to the VR-4.

One is a system that allows the driver to change the mechanical music coming from the car's dual exhaust by flicking a switch in the cockpit. In the VR-4's exhaust system, Mitsubishi has positioned a valve that can be opened or closed at speeds below 3,000rpm to restrict exhaust noise and power. Set the switch in the touring position, and the valve remains closed, greatly reducing exhaust noise and somewhat limiting power. In the sport mode, the valve is fully open and the exhaust note gets deeper and louder. Above 3,000rpm, the valve automatically closes because otherwise the exhaust noise could rise to illegal levels.

The other bit of technological cunning involves Mitsubishi's "active aero" system, a set-up that allows the front air dam and rear wing to change position as speed increases. At speeds rising above 50mph (80kmh), the front air dam drops down an additional 3.15in (8cm), and the cant of the rear wing increases 15 degrees at the same speed.

With all of these goodies crammed in, the Mitsubishi 3000GT VR-4 demanded aggressive styling. Working jointly with Chrysler's Highland Park International Design Studio, the stylists at Mitsubishi's studio in Okasaki, Japan, created a

BELOW: The 3000GT VR-4 is festooned with ducts and vent strakes, most of them functional.

MITSUBISHI 3000GT VR-4

RIGHT: A cut-away drawing reveals the technical wonders of the 3000GT VR-4.

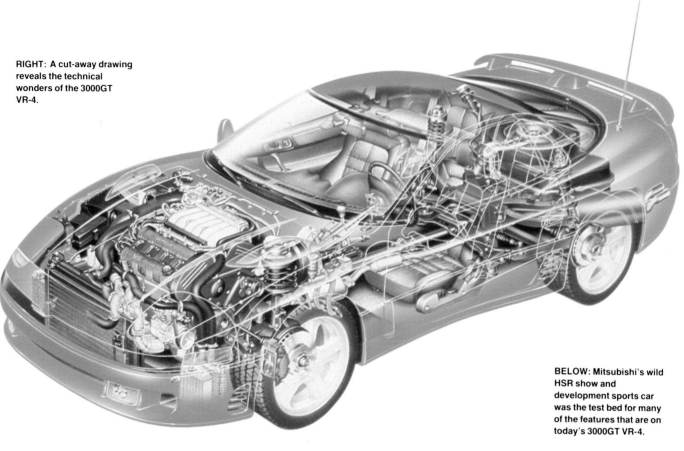

BELOW: Mitsubishi's wild HSR show and development sports car was the test bed for many of the features that are on today's 3000GT VR-4.

car that makes a definite performance statement. Influenced by the cab-forward styling of the HSR-II and Dodge Intrepid prototype vehicles, the 3000GT is awash in air dams, air scoops, vent ducts and power bulges. All are functional, but the rear side strakes that feed air to the rear disc brakes are undoubtedly there to remind people of the Ferrari Testarossa.

To some, the VR-4 may look a little too much like a California hot rod, lacking the smooth sophistication of Nissan's 300ZX. To the vast majority, however, the 3000GT oozes sex appeal in a way that only a high-performance car can.

Inside, the 3000GT VR-4 is surprisingly roomy at the front, though the vestigial back seats are hardly useful for anything more than carrying groceries. Seats in the VR-4 are fully adjustable and have high hip and back bolsters. They are covered in smooth leather, as are the door panels. Appointments throughout the cabin are high-grade, with the emphasis on utility with a heavy dose of sophistication.

ABOVE: The remarkable Mitsubishi HSR (High Speed Research) car has a body inspired by the contours of the tiny tropical humming bird.

BELOW: Seats on the 3000GT are very supportive, and the cockpit environment is geared towards aggressive driving.

ABOVE: The cab-forward design of the HSR-II prototype carried over into the production 3000GT.

RIGHT: Dashboard arrangement in the VR-4 is all business, with large gauges occupying centre stage.

The layout of the instruments is similar to the Nissan 280ZX from the 1980s, and is very driver-friendly. Two huge analogue dials – a 9000rpm tachometer and a 165mph (265kmh) speedo-meter – and a fuel gauge occupy the pod directly in front of the driver.

The adjustable steering column has an air-bag supplementary restraint system in the hub, which is lined at the bottom with remote radio controls. Three side stalks operate the cruise control, the lights and wipers.

In the centre is a secondary pod of instruments that relays information about the engine temp-erature, oil pressure and turbo boost.

The centre console, which flows down from the dashboard, contains the climate controls, as well as the AM/FM stereo cassette system and the optional compact disc player.

The air-conditioning and heating system uses a computer display to set the temperature and air flow. Using red and orange figures, a screen shows where the vents are going to direct the air and displays the desired temperature setting.

Above the leather-wrapped gear stick knob is an extra touch that is Mitsubishi's acknowledge-ment that we live in a very electronic era. In addi-tion to the usual cigarette lighter, the 3000GT provides a second power port where a driver can conveniently plug in a radar detector or some other necessary portable appliance.

Finally, at its list price of about $34,000 (£20,000), affordable sophistication – and speed – is what the 3000GT VR-4 is all about.

SPECIFICATIONS

DIMENSIONS

Wheelbase: 97.2in (246.88cm)
Overall length: 180.5in (458.47cm)
Width: 72.4in (183.90cm)
Height: 49.1in (124.71cm)
Front Track: 61.4in (155.96cm)
Rear Track: 62.2in (157.99cm)
Weight: 3,750lb (1,702.5kg)
Fuel capacity: 19.8gall (74.95l)

ENGINE

24-valve, DOHC V-6
Iron block, aluminium heads, multipoint fuel injection
Twin intercooled turbochargers
Bore and Stroke: 3.59 × 2.99in (9.12 × 7.59cm)
Displacement: 2972cc
Compression Ratio: 8.0:1
Horsepower: Net 296bhp @ 5500rpm
Torque: Net 307lb-ft @ 2500rpm
Redline: 7000rpm

GEARBOX

Five-speed Getrag manual
Gear ratios: (1) 3.07 (2) 1.74 (3) 1.10 (4) 0.82 (5) 0.70
Rear end ratio: 3.97:1

SUSPENSION

Independent front with damper struts, lower control arms, coil springs and anti-roll bar
Independent rear with upper and lower semi-trailing arms, lower transverse links, coil springs and anti-roll bar

STEERING

Rack and pinion
Variable ratio, power-assisted

BRAKES

Power-assisted four-wheel discs
Disc size: 16.0in (40.64cm) front, 15.0in (38.10cm) rear
Computer-controlled anti-lock system

WHEELS AND TYRES

17 × 8.5in (43.18 × 21.59cm) cast aluminium wheels
245/45ZR-17 Goodyear "Gatorback" Eagle radials

DRIVING IMPRESSIONS

The experience of driving the 3000GT VR-4 begins even before you open the door to slide behind the wheel. Just running your eyes over the aggressive, voluptuous shape of the VR-4 gives you a heady feeling. The "no-holes-barred" look of the car – which appeals to many but may be a bit too much for a few – is just a prelude to what the car offers when it's cranked up.

Once inside the cockpit, the feel of the very supportive leather seats reaffirms the exterior's statement, though the few drawbacks of the 3000GT make themselves apparent from the driver's seat. Many of the car's auxiliary controls are poorly placed, the computer screen that monitors the cockpit air-flow is difficult to read in daylight and the pod-mounted gauges are too small to be read quickly at speed.

But once the twin-turbo V-6 is fired up and the buttery-smooth Getrag five-speed gearbox is engaged, the overall first impression of this car is that it is an amazing engineering accomplishment. The power comes on instantly and there is almost no turbo lag. The 60mph (96.5kmh) mark on the speedometer comes up in about five seconds and then is forgotten as the 3000GT just keeps accelerating.

Gear changes are positive with no fiddling around to find the right gear, and the clutch is light with a short-travel pedal. Take a turn fast, and the 3000GT makes you feel like a Grand Prix driver, it is so predictable and forgiving. There is a slight twitchy feel to the steering at very high speed, but it's easy to overcome and at no time does it threaten the car's handling.

Mitsubishi's all-wheel-drive system operates so well most drivers will never know that all four wheels are putting down power. There is no torque-steer from the front wheels and on slippery surfaces that all-wheel-drive system makes the 3000GT far more sure-footed than most cars with nearly 300 horsepower. Huge disc brakes can bring the 3000GT down from top speeds time and time again without any bother.

However, several of the gimmicks that Mitsubishi's engineers added to the VR-4 – the speed-sensitive aero package and the adjustable exhaust – offer little real-world usefulness. At high speeds, the movement of the air dam at the front and the wing at the back seem from the driver's seat to do little to enhance stability or performance. And the cockpit-adjustable exhaust system is only of value if you live in an area with very tight noise restrictions.

Another note of caution: do not confuse the lesser-grade Mitsubishi 3000GTs with the VR-4 model. Without the trick engine and the all-wheel drive that are at the heart of the VR-4 package, the 3000GT is a much more pedestrian vehicle. In the VR-4 mode, however, the Mitsubishi 3000GT is a world-class sports car that rivals – and sometimes exceeds – the best Europe and America has to offer, at a price that makes it a true bargain.

NISSAN 300ZX TURBO

TOP SPEED: 155mph (249kmh)

ACCELERATION: 0 to 60mph in 5.5 seconds

ENGINE: Turbocharged three-litre, 24-valve DOHC V-6

HORSEPOWER: 300bhp @ 6400rpm

Supple in shape, steeped in tradition and loaded with power, Nissan's Turbo 300ZX is a rocketship on wheels. When the twin turbochargers kick in and propel the ZX's slick profile through the atmosphere, it's like a ride on the Space Shuttle.

NISSAN 300 ZX スポーツカー

日本のスポーツカー

If history and pedigrees count for anything, Nissan's 300ZX is the most venerable of all Japanese sports cars. When the model was introduced in 1970 as the 240Z, it was a revolutionary idea – a sports car that performed well, looked great and was as reliable as any car on the road.

From that solid base, Nissan gradually improved on the Z car. Although there were a few hiccups – the 260Z was perhaps the least successful version – each successive Z was an improved, more sophisticated car, representing Nissan's perception of what drivers wanted.

When more power was the order of the day, Nissan added turbocharging; when luxury touches were required, the 280ZX was rolled out; when a rudimentary back seat was needed, a 2+2 model was added; when open-air driving became popular, a T-bar roof with removable panels was incorporated into the design. By the late 1980s, when the perception was that drivers wanted a boulevard car that looked good but was not too aggressive, the initial 300ZX was the perfect answer to that equation.

That was the history that Nissan engineers and stylists had behind them when they began to consider just what sort of Z car they would create for the 1990s. They also faced a market-place that was changing and becoming more competitive all the time.

Chevrolet's Corvette had been improving steadily, and by 1990 had evolved into a sports car that offered superb power and handling. Porsche, a spiritual if not actual competitor, had also honed its 944 series into a row of potent sports cars, and the promise of even better Porsches was on the horizon.

Nissan's Japanese competitors were not to be taken lightly either. Mazda was hard at work on massive improvements to its RX-7 range – although the new rotary-engined cars did not appear until 1992. Honda was about to introduce its top-drawer NSX supercar, and Mitsubishi had its incredible 3000GT VR-4 waiting in the wings.

The challenge that Nissan faced was to create a new 300ZX that would be a contender in all aspects, from performance to styling to comfort. With so many good sports car choices available to buyers, the market-place demanded an all-out effort for the new 300ZX. Nissan responded admirably by starting with a blank computer screen and designing its new Z car with few if any compromises.

Starting with the body, Nissan made a quantum leap away from its most recent 300ZX, which had a look that many felt was too chunky and cumbersome for a sports car. The new Z was sculpted with flowing lines and a proportioning that suggests a mid-engined design, rather than the front-engined layout that it really uses.

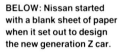

BELOW: Nissan started with a blank sheet of paper when it set out to design the new generation Z car.

ABOVE: Nissan's Fairlady for the 1980s was the third generation of this type, and used a massively powerful turbocharged V6 engine. Styling was strictly homegrown, and the car was sold in 2 + 2 or two-seater guise.

The wheelbase of the car was increased by 5in (12.7cm), while the overall length was shortened by nearly 4in (10cm) and the width increased by 2⅔in (6.5cm). The result is a car with very little front and rear overhang, and a squat stance that exudes sex appeal.

The front end is a marvellous marriage of form and function. Designers wanted to create a car with a low drag coefficient, yet they had to cater to all the cooling needs of a high-performance engine. Nissan engineers used a Cray supercomputer to overcome those sometimes conflicting demands.

Rather than resort to the time-honoured tradition of pop-up headlights, Nissan kept the front end profile low by using new optical breakthroughs that allowed the headlights to be laid back at a 60-degree angle. The overall drag coefficient of 0.31 was also achieved by pushing the wheels out to the extent that they are flush with the Z's bodywork.

Elsewhere, the design of the Z is equally well executed. The sail panels that run from the cockpit to the tail are sleek and combine well with the sharp arrangement of the tail-lights, which are recessed into a blacked-out panel.

As a whole, the 300ZX styling is reminiscent of a few Ferrari designs, yet is refreshing and unique. Nissan could have stopped there, and the 300ZX would have been a hit when it was introduced in 1990. But to be an enduring player in the sports car game takes more than just a superb body

shape, and Nissan engineers made sure the rest of the Z was as beautiful as the coachwork.

The chassis is as innovative as the 300ZX styling. As a starting point, engineers conceived of a new unibody structure that was dramatically stronger than the old Z cars. That gave the suspension experts an extremely stable platform on which to build. One of the goals was to build a suspension that would react differently to all the assorted demands that might be made upon it. While some manufacturers are experimenting with complex computers to achieve this, Nissan resorted to some shrewd engineering to build a suspension that adjusts itself to cornering, braking and acceleration.

The front kingpin on each wheel, for example, is controlled at the bottom and top by two-piece linkages that separate the functions of camber, caster, steering offset and anti-roll. That means that when the 300ZX is moving in a straight line, there is no camber change and the contact patch of the tyre remains at right angles to the road. And when the tyre is turned in a cornering manoeuvre, the multiple offset suspension arms crank in more camber to keep the rubber in the optimum right-angle position. At the back, the multilink system does much the same thing, producing desired toe-in when the situation demands it. On top of this, the shock absorbers can be remotely cranked down into a super-stiff mode via a switch in the cockpit.

If the actions of all these complex parts were put on a graph, there would be a mass of arcs and axes showing what the car was being asked to do. Nissan again turned to its Cray supercomputer to work out the geometry in all of this so that the system works flawlessly.

This is the suspension that is standard on the normally aspirated 300ZX. When the twin-turbo engine is installed, Nissan adds its Super HICAS – High-Capacity Actively Controlled Suspension. Super HICAS is a four-wheel steering system that enhances high-speed directional changes by cranking in a slight same-phase, toe-in at the rear wheels. With the standard suspension and the extra frosting of the Super HICAS steering system on the 300ZX Turbo. Nissan has created a chassis that is a leader in the field.

Equally intelligent is the speed-sensitive power steering on the 300ZX. Rather than stay with the standard method of enhancing road feel – decreasing the assist at speed by limiting the fluid flow on the hydraulic system – Nissan made a significant improvement. In a standard system, a driver can be put off using steering boost if a sudden manoeuvre is required at high speed. With the 300ZX, the power steering relies on a two-stage system that keeps sufficient fluid flowing so that sudden demands don't find the system momentarily caught off guard.

Rounding off the chassis are four-wheel disc brakes that are vented and use aluminium callipers to reduce the unsprung weight at each corner. A computer-controlled anti-lock system is also included.

When it comes to engine power, the 300ZX can be had in "hot" and "red-hot" forms. Although the V-6 engine in the new 300ZX is the same displacement as the last car, it is much more sophisticated. In non-turbo form, the 60-degree V-6 uses 24 valves, four overhead camshafts, aluminium cylinder heads and innovative induction and valve train modifications to produce 222 horsepower from 2960cc of displacement.

Among the methods Nissan used to get the most power from this engine are tuned intake runners and flow-enhanced cylinder ports. Also, there is no central spark distributor, since each cylinder gets its own compact coil to fire the spark plug. Optimum combustion is also enhanced by a system called NVTC – Nissan Valve Timing Control – which mechanically adjusts the valve timing for maximum intake and exhaust at different engine speeds. The result of all this is a very smooth V-6 that hits its peak horsepower at 6400rpm, and delivers 198 foot-pounds of torque at 4800rpm.

As amazing as this engine is, it pales by comparison to the twin-turbo version Nissan puts in the top-of-the-line 300ZX. Before giving details of all that goes into the turbo engine, it is worth noting that Nissan managed to fit a lot of hardware under the sharply tapered aluminium bonnet of the standard 300ZX. There is a place for everything, so there was no need to spoil the smooth lines of the Z car's nose. So it's even more impressive that all the components associated with a turbocharged engine were made to fit as well without having to resort to bulges on the bonnet.

BELOW: Turbo technology that helped Nissan get 300 horsepower from the twin-turbo Z car was pioneered on the GTP cars.

ABOVE: The engineers managed to keep the low profile of the 300ZX and yet find room for all the plumbing required for the turbocharged engine.

To enhance the standard three-litre engine, Nissan attached a pair of modified Garrett turbochargers that produce 9lb (4.08kg) of pressure at their peak. The two units are cooled by a system that uses both oil and water, and draw fresh air from two intercoolers that are mounted low in the nose and connect to intakes below the turn signal/foglight cluster.

The interior of the iron-block Z engine is strengthened to handle the demands of the turbochargers. Special aluminium pistons, connecting rod bearings and aircraft-strength steel exhaust valves are added, and the compression ratio is cut back from a normal 10.5 to 8.5:1. The Z's turbo engine produces an amazing 300 horsepower – 100 horses per litre – at 6400rpm. Torque is a very strong 283 foot-pounds at a very low 3600rpm. Top speed for a turbocharged 300ZX is limited by an engine governor to 155mph (249.39kmh), though contemporary road tests suggest 165mph (265.49kmh) or better would be possible.

Either 300ZX is available with a choice of a five-speed manual gearbox or a four-speed automatic overdrive gearbox. The five-speed unit benefits from new double-cone synchronizers that equalize the effort required to change gears, and on the turbo version the gearsets for second and fifth gears are strengthened. Also, turbo ZXs come with a clutch with 38 per cent more capacity and a vacuum assist on the pedal. The automatic gearbox is the same in both cars, but the turbo engine is dialed back to 280 horsepower to provide a smoother marriage to the gearbox.

Another area that undergoes a change when the turbo engine is specified are the wheels and tyres. On the normally aspirated ZX, all four tyres are 225/50VR models mounted on 16 × 7.5in (40.6 × 19.1cm) aluminium wheels. For the faster

RIGHT: While the design of the 300ZX is evolutionary, it makes a very sharp styling statement. Viewed from the back, the ZX almost appears to be a mid-engine design.

SPECIFICATIONS

DIMENSIONS

Wheelbase: 96.5in (245.11cm)
Overall length: 169.5in (430.53cm)
Width: 70.5in (179.07cm)
Height: 49.2in (124.97cm)
Front Track: 58.9in (149.61cm)
Rear Track: 61.2in (155.45cm)
Weight: 3,474lb (1,577.20kg)
Fuel capacity: 18.7gall (70.79l)

ENGINE

24-valve, DOHC V-6
Iron block and aluminium cylinder heads
Multipoint electronic fuel injection
Garrett AiResearch T25 turbochargers
Bore and Stroke: 3.43 × 3.27in (8.71 × 8.31cm)
Displacement: 2960cc
Compression Ratio: 8.5:1
Horsepower: Net 300bhp @ 6400rpm
Torque: Net 283lb-ft @ 3600rpm
Redline: 7000rpm

GEARBOX

Five-speed manual overdrive
Gear ratios: (1) 3.21 (2) 1.93 (3) 1.30 (4) 1.00 (5) 0.75
Rear end ratio: 3.69:1

SUSPENSION

Four-wheel independent
Lower A-arm with dual upper links at the front
Upper and lower control arms with trailing link at back
Coil springs
Front and rear anti-roll bars

STEERING

Rack and pinion, variable ratio, power-assisted
Turns, lock-to-lock: 2.4
Turning circle: 34.1ft (10.39m)

BRAKES

Power-assisted four-wheel discs with anti-lock
Disc size: 11.0in (27.94cm) front, 11.7in (29.72cm) rear

WHEELS AND TYRES

Cast aluminium wheels, 16×7.5in (40.64× 19.05cm) front, 16×8.5in (40.64×21.59cm) rear
Michelin MXX, 225/50ZR-16 front, 245/45ZR-16 rear

RIGHT: It's a tribute to the
design of the 300ZX that it
retains its shape even
when it's stretched to
accommodate 2 + 2
seating.

turbo, the tyres are upgraded to a Z rating – which means they can sustain a constant speed of more than 150mph (241.35kmh) – and the rear wheels and tyres grow to 245/45ZR models mounted on 16 × 8.5in (40.6 × 21.6cm) wheels.

What doesn't change from turbo to non-turbo on the 300ZX is the superb interior that the ergonomic experts created for the new generation car. Starting a trend that began with Nissan's new 240SX and the Maxima sports sedan, the ZX has an interior that is geared solely towards making sure the necessary controls are at the driver's fingertips. Using a system of pods, Nissan has positioned just about every control in the vicinity of the steering wheel. In front of the driver is a pod of instruments dominated by a large white-on-black speedometer and tachometer, and smaller but equally readable gauges for all other engine functions.

To the immediate right of the instrument cluster are controls for the climate-control system and the windscreen wipers. To the left of the instru-

ment cluster is a pod that contains a number of switches for lights, cruise control and rear-window defroster.

The centre console contains two air-conditioning vents, the stereo system, the gear stick and the switch for the sport suspension mode. Mounted on the door panels are window and door-lock controls, as well as additional air-conditioning vents.

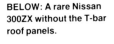

BELOW: A rare Nissan
300ZX without the T-bar
roof panels.

Seating is very firm and there are high bolsters on the seat bottom and back to make sure the driver and passenger stay put under hard cornering. In the 2 + 2 configuration, two small back seats are added so that children can be accommodated on short journeys. In standard trim, the seats are covered in a handsome and serviceable cloth, accented by vinyl. However, leather is an option, as are power seats, heated outside mirrors, an automatic temperature-control system as well as a Bose-designed stereo with added compact disc player.

Those who buy their 300ZX outside the United States get a choice of a hardtop or removable T-tops. For the US market, Nissan is only offering the T-top version. The removable panels are easy to lift off and install, and they are relatively light.

Given the high technology found in the 300ZX, its price is somewhat surprising. The normally aspirated version has a base price of about $28,000 (£16,470), and the turbo's base price is about $34,000 (£20,000). The package that includes the Bose stereo and the automatic climate control adds about $1,600 (£940), and leather seats can add another $1,000 (£588) to the price. Still, a fully loaded 300ZX will cost far less than $40,000 (£23,530), and significantly less than its European competitors. This is where Nissan shows the edge the Japanese bring to the market; they offer a world-class sports car in the 300ZX at a price that few can match.

ABOVE: Very few outward details distinguish a turbocharged Z from the tamer but still potent 222-horsepower version shown here.

DRIVING IMPRESSIONS

The first sentence I want to write about driving the Nissan 300ZX Turbo is that it is a perfect, expensive, affordable sports car. Now I know that those three words – perfect, expensive, and affordable – don't normally go together, but on the 300ZX they do.

First, let's look at why the adjective perfect applies to the 300ZX. From just about any angle, it's very hard to find fault with the ZX. Its styling works so well that there is not a single element that's out of place, and the overall shape is very seductive. It turns heads wherever it goes, and that's a measure of perfection in a sports car.

Another measure is in handling, and the 300ZX is as forgiving a car as has ever been built. Its suspension keeps the driver in full control of where the car is going, regardless of driving conditions. It has great poise on rough roads, is stable in straight lines, and can be pushed to the limit in curves without any shocking surprises. Make no mistake, the 300ZX is no featherweight car. It is not light on its feet, but the suspension works so well it doesn't matter that it weighs almost 3,500lb (1,589kg). The handling is so good, the 300ZX can instantly improve the skills of just about any driver.

And then there is that turbocharged engine. When it comes to producing great amounts of power and doing it smoothly, the 300ZX Turbo has few equals in its price range. Anyone who has driven a turbocharged car has come to expect a trade-off for all that power – the dreaded turbo lag, when there is a perceptible wait between the time the accelerator is pressed and the time the engine responds. Nissan has virtually eliminated turbo lag in the 300ZX. Power comes on just above idle and stays on until the redline is reached. From a stop, the turbo ZX can hit 60mph (96.54kmh) in just 5.5 seconds.

Other areas of the car are just as pleasing, such as the brakes, the interior and the fit and finish.

However, all this greatness comes at significant expense. Any car that costs about $35,000 (£20,586) cannot be considered a cheap set of wheels. And a hidden cost down the road – far down the road, if Nissan is up to its usual reliability standards – will come when those complex systems in the engine and suspension need repairing or replacing. The 300ZX requires a specialist mechanic, so it is going to be a very costly car to keep running properly when the odometer kicks past the 100,000-mile (160,000km) mark.

Nonetheless, taken as an overall package of style, handling, performance and sophistication, the 300ZX Turbo is a car that is too affordable to pass up. Probably never again will a sports car this perfect be offered new at this price. Snap one up, drive it for 60,000 miles (95,000km) and then trade it in. It will be the most perfect experience of your motoring life.

MAZDA MX-5 MIATA

TOP SPEED: 117mph (188kmh)

ACCELERATION: 0 to 60mph in 8.6 seconds

ENGINE: 1.6-litre, 16-valve DOHC in-line four

HORSEPOWER: 116bhp @ 6500rpm

In looks and reliability the Mazda's MX-5 Miata is the car everyone wants. In an era when too many cars have forgotten their roots, the Miata gets back to basics — the basics that all supercar fans crave.

ロ MAZDA ⒨ MX-5 ㋹ MIATA ツーカー

日本のスポーツカー

There are a significant number of people in the world today who believe everything is just too complex. They can't programme their video cassette recorders, their microwave ovens seem cleverer than they are, and their cars have become so unfathomable that they are afraid to open up the bonnet. Then there are people who cope very well with 1990s' technology, but they yearn for the days when machines were simpler, particularly cars.

Mazda built a sports car in 1989 to appeal to all of those people and others who wanted a car that was as much fun as the British sports cars of the 1960s. Called the Mazda MX-5 Miata – or just Miata for short – it was a marketing and engineering *tour de force* that stunned the motoring world. Simply put, Mazda studied the characteristics of cars such as the MGB, the Triumph TR4 and the Lotus Elan, kept the good parts, threw out the bad, and created the Miata.

At a base price of just $13,800 (£8,118), the Miata was the first affordable sports car in more than a decade. It was such a success that thousands of people literally queued to buy one, jaded motoring journalists drooled over it and industry observers said it was one of the most significant cars since the 1964 Ford Mustang. Newspapers devoted front-page space to "Miata Mania" that swept through the United States.

People talked about how much fun the car was to drive, how sweet it looked, how heads turned wherever it went. And they talked about how they were willing to pay hefty premiums over the manufacturer's list price to get one. Dealers, particularly in California, charged as much as $10,000 (£5,882) over list price to eager buyers. And some buyers, who were lucky enough to find a dealer who would sell the Miata at something near list price, promptly turned around and resold their cars at a profit.

In some cities, people would trail the Mazda delivery truck as it drove to the dealer, then rush in to buy the Miata on board before it was backed off the truck. Eventually, as supply and demand equalized at about 40,000 cars a year, the hysteria subsided. Yet today the Miata remains a coveted car, with a status equal to cars costing three times as much.

So what is this car that has excited so many people? Looked at cynically, the Miata is just a two-seater, four-cylinder convertible. In reality, it may be the best pure sports car ever built.

Mazda was no stranger to building sports cars when it first began to plan the Miata in the late 1980s. The RX-7, which uses the innovative Wankel rotary engine for power, is a well-respected player in the sports car field. But as its price and sophistication grew, along with such competitors

BELOW: When the Miata made its debut, it spawned a new description for such simple new cars – Retrotech.

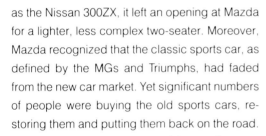

as the Nissan 300ZX, it left an opening at Mazda for a lighter, less complex two-seater. Moreover, Mazda recognized that the classic sports car, as defined by the MGs and Triumphs, had faded from the new car market. Yet significant numbers of people were buying the old sports cars, restoring them and putting them back on the road.

To find out what the appeal of these relics was, several MGs, Triumphs and Lotuses were shipped to Japan for evaluation. After they were dissected, a list of their attributes was made and Mazda engineers set out to duplicate them in a new car. First on that list was the acknowledgement that any pure sports car had to have a small, responsive engine that was linked to the rear wheels. Mazda had the perfect sports car engine mounted in its sporty saloon, the 323. Known by the Mazda nomenclature as B6-ZE, the 1.6-litre in-line four-cylinder used twin overhead camshafts and four valves per cylinder to generate 116 horsepower at 6500rpm.

Although the engine is used in a transverse position to drive the Mazda 323's front wheels, for the Miata it would fit snugly in a more conventional front-to-back position, which was the way it was done in the 1960s. To further the imagery, the valve covers on the 1.6-litre engine were sculpted to look similar to the Lotus Elan's twin-cam engine. The engine was linked to the rear wheels by a five-speed manual gearbox that uses closely spaced ratios to take advantage of the engine's high-revving nature. As a concession to the realities of modern city driving, a four-speed automatic is a Miata option.

TOP LEFT: Despite its relatively skinny tyres, the Miata has a wide stance on the road.

BELOW: Engine valve covers were crafted to resemble the twin-cam Ford engine found in the 1960s Lotus Elan.

ABOVE: Crisp handling, a lively engine and irresistible styling are what make the Miata a world-class car.

The gearbox is mounted on an alloy beam that isolates the drivetrain from the body and interior. That set-up was used so that the assembly gave the Miata a very low centre of gravity as well as a near 50/50 front-rear weight distribution.

That accomplished, the engineers set out to provide a suspension that mirrored the sports car feel, yet was compliant enough to handle the rough roads of today. Because of the chassis' low centre of gravity and near-perfect weight distribution, Mazda was able to use a suspension that doesn't have to rely on very tight springs and computer-controlled shock absorbers to keep the Miata under control. The Miata rides on a wishbone-design suspension that uses low-mounted upper and lower A-arms at the front, along with moderately soft coil springs, gas shock absorbers and an anti-roll bar. At the rear is a nearly identical set-up that uses unequal bushing elasticity to generate a certain amount of toe-in under hard cornering.

In an almost monocoque approach to construction, the suspension is aided by the tight nature of the body assembly. Mazda used computer analysis to monitor 8,900 points on the body

shell for flex and shake under simulated road conditions. Armed with that information, the engineers bolstered the Miata to make it as solid as possible, yet keep the weight down to about 2,100lb (953.4kg).

When it came to styling the Miata body shell, Mazda did not sway from its goal of making a car that was true to the classic definition of a sports car. It had to be a convertible with just two seats and an overall jaunty air to it. With the help of stylists at Mazda's Southern California design studio, the Miata's shape was hammered out.

Looking at a tape measure, the Miata compares favourably to the 1963 MGB, the car that for many was the ultimate expression of the British sports machine. The Miata is 48.2in (122.43cm) high, just an inch (2.50cm) lower than the MGB, is more than 2in (5cm) longer overall and rides on a wheelbase that is just fractions of an inch shorter than the MG. The only dimension where the comparison wavers is in terms of width, where the Miata is 65.9in (167.39cm) across, compared to 59.8in (151.89cm) for the MGB.

Although dimensionally the Miata is akin to the MGB, its overall styling owes much more to the

1965 Lotus Elan in terms of its rounded nose, tail and fenders and its pop-up headlights. But Colin Chapman's Elan could not have been built in this day and age of crash-resistant bumpers, so it is a tribute to the Mazda stylists that they were able to conceive of a shape that evokes memories of the Elan yet remains modern.

The British-era look is also continued in the wheels and tyres of the Miata. The seven-spoke alloy wheels are strongly reminiscent of the Mini-lites that many sports cars used in the 1960s, and the 185/60R-14 tyres are wide enough to provide sufficient grip, yet a lot narrower than the modern trend towards fat, super-low-profile tyres.

Inside the cockpit is where the Miata shows its Japanese roots. In keeping with its minimalist design goals, the Miata's interior provides enough instrumentation and controls to get the job done. The driver faces a hooded gauge pod that contains two large white-on-black dials for speed and engine revs, and smaller gauges for fuel, temperature and oil pressure.

An air bag – a necessary concession – is housed in the four-spoke steering wheel, and two stalks take care of indicators, lights, windscreen wipers and the optional cruise control.

Two round, adjustable vents – which are among four that circulate air throughout the cockpit – dominate the centre control panel. Below these vents are the simple, easily read controls for the heater and optional air-conditioning, and the standard AM/FM stereo cassette sound system.

The gear stick rises up to become a substantial divider between the two cloth-and-vinyl deep bucket seats, which have manual adjustments for repositioning. Behind the seats is a padded shelf where the convertible top, when lowered, folds up, meaning that any luggage must fit in the rudimentary boot.

Speaking of the top, that's an area where the Mazda engineers found plenty of room for improvement. It was a common complaint in the 1960s that sports car folding tops tended to leak and were hard to put up and down. One of the Miata design goals was to make a top that could be raised and lowered with one hand by someone sitting in the driver's seat. Also, the top had to seal tightly to the windscreen frame at speeds of up to at least 80mph (128.7kmh). Using large, centre-mounted clamps, the Miata has exceptional tightness when the top is up. For really cold and inclement weather, an optional hardtop

LEFT: Cooling air is fed to the 1.8-litre engine through a large opening below the front bumper.

is available, but it too is of a simple, unlined lightweight design.

Options on the Miata when it was introduced were few and very basic. Air-conditioning, an upgraded stereo, cruise control, power steering and an automatic gear box were among the few extras that were offered. And initially Miata owners had to be content with either a red, white or blue car, and all interiors came in black. Later, silver was added to the list, and in 1991 Mazda came out with its first special edition, which sported British Racing Green paint and a tan leather interior. In addition to the paint and interior, the BRG model had a wood-rim steering wheel and shift knob, as well as the option of anti-lock brakes and power windows. Only 4,000 of the green Miatas were built, and forecourt prices were about $21,000 (£12,350) – though many Mazda dealers once again took advantage of buyer demand and added on high price premiums.

Looking at its component parts, it is hard to believe the Miata is a supercar. Its engine is a fine, tightly built unit that produces enough horse-power to move the Miata along briskly; but its top speed of 117mph (188.25kmh) is nothng to brag about. Its suspension is well engineered, but it uses no computers or space-age alloys. Its cock-pit is well appointed, yet it is small and there's not a computer display to be seen anywhere. Its styling is clean and handsome, yet it is also mild-mannered: "sweet" is the operative word.

But Mazda wasn't looking for a cutting-edge car when it created the Miata. The engineers and product planners recognized that other things besides all-out speed and design were what made sports cars fun. For example, Mazda knew that a large degree of the fun found in sports cars of the 1960s was sensory based. People loved the feel of the wind and the noises associated with open-air driving.

BELOW: Dark green paint gives the special edition Miata a very British flavour.

ABOVE: Pop-up headlights give the Miata a look that is similar to the Frog-Eye Sprite from the late 1950s.

Towards that end, Mazda engineers worked on making sure there was enough breeze blowing through the Miata cockpit when the top was down, yet not so much that it was annoying. Also, they decided that a sports car got its distinctive sound from a combination of engine and exhaust noise. So they tuned the engine and the silencer to just the right pitch.

RIGHT: Mazda engineers tested the cockpit environment of convertibles so they could devise ways to keep interior turbulence to a minimum.

They knew that one big reason the affordable sports car disappeared was because buyers grew weary of their cars not starting in the morning, of overheating problems, of mystical electrical failures and the myriad other foibles associated with cars such as the MG, the Triumph and the Lotus. So what they delivered in the Miata was a car that looked and acted like a sports car, yet was as reliable as the most mundane saloon on the road. It was a revolutionary idea, and that is what makes the Miata one of the world's best sports cars.

FAR RIGHT: Big gauges and simple controls mark the dashboard of the Miata.

SPECIFICATIONS

DIMENSIONS

Wheelbase: 89.2in (226.57cm)
Overall length: 155.4in (394.72cm)
Width: 65.9in (167.39cm)
Height: 48.2in (122.43cm)
Front Track: 55.5in (140.97cm)
Rear Track: 56.2in (142.75cm)
Weight: 2,189lb (993.81kg)
Fuel capacity: 11.9gall (45.05l)

ENGINE

16-valve, DOHC in-line four
Iron block with aluminium heads
Electronic fuel injection
Bore and Stroke: 3.07 × 3.29in (7.80 × 8.36cm)
Displacement: 1597cc
Compression Ratio: 9.4:1
Horsepower: Net 116bhp @ 6500rpm
Torque: Net 100lb-ft @ 5500rpm
Redline: 7000rpm

GEARBOX

Five-speed manual
Gear ratios: (1) 3.14 (2) 1.89 (3) 1.33 (4) 1.00 (5) 0.81
Rear end ratio: 4.30:1

SUSPENSION

Four-wheel independent
Upper and lower A-arms
Coil springs
Gas-pressurized shock absorbers
Front and rear anti-roll bars

STEERING

Rack and pinion
Variable ratio, power-assisted (optional)

BRAKES

Power-assisted four-wheel discs
Disc size: 9.3in (23.62cm) front, 9.1in (23.11cm) rear
Computer-controlled anti-lock system (optional)

WHEELS AND TYRES

14 × 5.5in (35.56 × 13.97cm) cast aluminium wheels
185/60R-14 Bridgestone SF-325 tyres

A Miata pictured against
the imposing shape of
Hawaii's Diamondhead.

DRIVING IMPRESSIONS

When I was in my teens, an older friend told me that getting into a good sports car should feel a little like putting on your clothes. Not only should everything fit well, but it should feel comfortable and after a while it should fade into your skin. I was all of 16 years old, and the only cars I had driven were my father's Buick – which didn't fit my friend's definition – and my own Mustang convertible – which came a lot closer to the mark.

Getting into a Mazda Miata brings back those words of wisdom from more than 30 years ago. It simply feels like a sports car should. The door is small, but provides ample room to get into the driver's seat. Once the door is closed, the car seems to snuggle up to you, even when the top is down. The seats are very supportive, and the high transmission tunnel adds to the snug feel.

The wheel is positioned well, and it is designed not to obstruct the view of the large gauges – which look for all the world like the Smith's dials in the old British sports cars. The petrol, brake and clutch pedals are small, although there is ample room in the footwell. The gear stick is small and sits comfortably under your hand. It is a very neat set-up, and the stick moves between gears in a solid, reassuring way.

The 1.6-litre engine starts easily and has a very free-wheeling feel to it as the accelerator is touched. Once the gearbox is engaged and the revs rise above 1500, the Miata moves away smartly.

Speed in a Miata is a relative thing. Because it is so light and basic a car, a driver's relationship to the road and things around him are more intense. Consequently, 40mph (64.36kmh) tends to feel faster in a Miata than in, say, a Nissan 300ZX. Nevertheless, the Miata is pretty good when it comes to acceleration. Zero to 60mph (96.54kmh) takes about 8.6 seconds, and engine response is excellent. At most everyday speeds, the Miata begs you to put your foot to the floor.

Handling is an equal joy. The Miata goes where you point it and its suspension invites you to throw it into corners, a feeling that is lost in most heavier cars, even though they may have more capable suspensions than a Miata.

On the negative side, the Miata is a car that must be driven with the top down. When the roof is up, too much road noise can be heard in the cockpit, which makes long-distance driving unpleasant. With the top down, those unpleasant noises are replaced by glorious wind, engine and exhaust sounds that make the blood sing. After a few miles of top-down driving in the Miata, the driver and the car begin to feel like one, and – for a moment – it's not hard to imagine you're in the Mille Miglia.

MAZDA TWIN·TURBO RX·7

TOP SPEED: 155mph (249.44kmh)

ACCELERATION: 0 to 60mph in 5 seconds

ENGINE: Twin-turbocharged two-rotor 1.3-litre Wankel

HORSEPOWER: 255bhp @ 6500rpm

There's only one rotary-powered sports car in the world, and Mazda's got it. Its all-new shape is part of an all-business approach that stresses function over form. Under the bonnet is the most powerful production Wankel engine ever, and, combined with the new RX-7's lightweight chassis, it has helped Mazda to create a simple but fast supercar.

日 MAZDA RX-7 ポーツカー

Mazda RX-7: A Supercar With A Difference

日本のスポーツカー

ABOVE: The 1993 Mazda RX-7 – the only production car to use a rotary piston engine based on the design of Felix Wankel.

If you are looking for something truly different in supercar engines, then Mazda is the only place you can turn.

While Ferraris and Lamborghinis have their powerful V-12 engines, and cars like Lotus get their punch from high-output turbocharged four-cylinder engines, they all share one common trait – conventional piston engines. Those powerful engines trace their lineage back to the late nineteenth century when petrol piston-engine development began. The V-12s are also closely related to even the smallest economy-car engine, though a Ferrari Testarossa, for example, is obviously vastly more sophisticated.

Mazda's RX-7 sports car, on the other hand, moves to a different beat – or different hum, to be more accurate. And its latest incarnation, which has arrived as a 1993 model, can justifiably lay claim to supercar status.

The RX-7, which made its debut in 1978 as a 1979 model, is the only production car to use a rotary piston engine based on the design of German engineer Felix Wankel. In concept and execution, the Wankel engine has fewer parts and is lighter than a comparable up-and-down piston engine, yet offers more horsepower and is smoother. Early advertisements for rotary-engine cars stressed that they ran with a hum so quiet you could stand next to a car and not notice the engine was firing.

On paper it is a revolutionary engine, and in the 1950s, 60s and 70s it looked as though it would become the basis for the engines of the future. Yet Mazda, displaying the persistence and belief in their convictions that characterizes Japanese car makers, is the only manufacturer to have found a proper home for the engine in its sleek RX-7.

Rotary engines – in which the piston and the output shaft move in concentric circles – can be traced in theory to crude drawings as far back as the Middle Ages. By 1910 more than 2,000 patents were filed world-wide on the concept of a rotary. But it wasn't until Wankel began his work in the late 1920s in Heidelberg, Germany, that modern rotary-engine technology was born. Throughout the economic ruin of the 1930s and the devastation of the Second World War, Wankel pursued his rotary quest with varying degrees of success.

In the early 1950s, when Germany's shattered car industry was being revived, Wankel's dream of a rotary-engined car began to be realized. Eventually, NSU took on the rotary cause and built the first Wankel-engined production car, the Spider, in 1960 and the larger Ro80 in 1967.

Meanwhile, car makers as diverse as Mercedes-Benz, General Motors, Volkswagen and, of course, Mazda, paid Wankel hefty patent fees to develop their own rotary engines. Mercedes eventually developed an amazing four-rotor test car that produced 350 horsepower and could hit a top speed of 185mph (298kmh). Chevrolet produced a prototype Corvette that used a four-rotor Wankel as well.

Apart from NSU, Mazda was the first of the major car makers to put a rotary car on the market, in 1967 with its exotic and expensive Cosmos sports car.

However, most of the other rotary projects were never to see production. The Achilles' heel of early rotary engines was fuel consumption. Because of the way fuel is drawn into the three-chambered rotor, Wankels could not burn fuel as efficiently as in a conventional piston engine. By the early 1970s, when oil production was curtailed by world political turmoil, better petrol mileage was a rallying cry for car manufacturers and the rotary engine seemed destined to fail.

Mazda, however, didn't give up on the rotary. Bowing to the reality that the rotary was not to be the engine of choice for small economy cars, it eventually converted all its saloons to conventional piston engines. But Mazda engineers reasoned that there were types of cars where fuel economy could be traded for horsepower – namely sports cars.

So in 1978, Mazda unveiled its first RX-7, a small, nimble two-seater coupé that immediately became a hit. At a time when cars in general tended either to be little boxes without personalities or oversized dinosaurs awaiting extinction, the RX-7 was a refreshing idea. Though its two-rotor Wankel engine was small in displacement – about 1.2 litres – it produced 100 horsepower. Acceleration was spirited, but not overpowering. In fact, the first RX-7 exhibited many of the same characteristics as today's Mazda Miata.

As its competitors became more complex and added luxury features, the RX-7 followed suit. Throughout the 1980s, the RX-7 grew in size and power. A convertible was added, and the top-of-the-line model received the extra boost of turbo-charging in 1988. Under the hood Mazda remained true to the RX-7's roots and kept the Wankel rotary engine.

As a way of proving just how much respect its Wankel could command, Mazda also kept running its rotary cars in international races. That persistence paid off in 1991 when Mazda won the most prestigious sports car race in the world, the 24-hours of Le Mans. Its 787 four-rotor prototype outperformed Jaguar, Porsche and Mercedes,

despite being saddled with extra weight and re-fuelling restrictions allegedly imposed to put the Wankel on an even footing with its more conventional competitors.

That watershed victory – the first for a Japanese manufacturer – was a fitting harbinger for the latest generation of RX-7, which at once returns the sports car to its lightweight roots and yet embodies the sophistication of the 1990s. Leaving its rotary engine on one side for a moment, the 1993 RX-7 is a car whose concept has been re-worked entirely.

ABOVE: Because of its light weight and ideal 50/50 weight distribution, the RX-7 is a nimble sports car.

BELOW: Despite restrictions on fuel stops, Mazda won Le Mans by a wide margin.

Conventional wisdom in the 1980s held that high-performance sports cars had to be almost equal mixes of acceleration and luxury. That resulted in cars that were fast, but heavy for their size. The RX-7 was no exception, tipping the scales at more than 3,000 pounds (1,362kg) and accelerating to 60mph (96.5kmh) in just 6.7 seconds. Though the cars were competent in the handling department, nimble was a word that rarely came up in a description of an RX-7's handling characteristics.

When they set out to create a third-generation RX-7, Mazda engineers determined that their sports car needed to be slimmed down, and become at once both simpler and more powerful. So they designed a new steel space-monocoque frame on which to build the new RX-7. The new frame is significantly lighter than the unibody design it replaces, is 20 per cent more rigid and is easier to build on the Hiroshima assembly line.

The suspension design is an independent double wishbone arrangement at the front and the rear uses coil springs, gas-filled shock absorbers and anti-roll bars. Steering is a power-assisted rack-and-pinion set-up that is speed-sensitive. Mazda says it responds to driver input at a speed of 1/100th of a second – about the same time it takes a human muscle to react. Brakes are large 11.6-in (29.5-cm) discs with four-piston calipers at the front, and a single-piston set-up at the rear. An anti-lock computer system is standard. Wheels are eight-inch-wide (20.3cm) aluminium alloy rims allied with 225/50-16 radial tyres. Front-to-rear weight distribution is a perfect 50/50 balance, which helps keep the handling stable.

Compared to other cars in its class, the new RX-7 is devoid of a number of high-tech features. There is no four-wheel steering, no all-wheel-drive, no computer-assisted suspension, no electronically tuned exhaust. That's in keeping

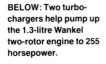

BELOW: Two turbo-chargers help pump up the 1.3-litre Wankel two-rotor engine to 255 horsepower.

with Mazda's new philosophy regarding the RX-7: it will be a "pure sports car" that will use a favourable weight-to-horsepower ratio to maximum advantage.

Much of that advantage will come from the new twin-turbocharged rotary engine under the hood. The power plant, dubbed 13B-STT in Mazda nomenclature, is the most powerful rotary engine ever put into production. Although it displaces the same 1.3 litres as the RX-7 engine it replaces, it produces 255 horsepower at 6,500rpm – more than 70 horsepower above the old turbocharged rotary engine. Torque is an equally impressive 217foot-pounds at 5,000rpm, up from 183foot-pounds in the old engine.

When the RX-7's light weight is taken into account – curb weight is just 2,800lb (1,271kg) – it falls in with some heady company. The RX-7 produces an 11-to-1 weight-to-horsepower ratio. That compares to a 10.3-to-1 ratio for a Ferrari 348. To get all that horsepower from the tiny Wankel, Mazda used a variety of tricks taken from racing. Two sequential intercooled turbochargers are employed, as is a Bosch D-Jetronic electronic fuel-injection system and a distributor-

less timing system. The compression ratio is set at 9.0-to-1, and the engine runs on regular unleaded petrol. Power is transmitted to the rear wheels through either a five-speed manual gearbox or a four-speed automatic system.

When it comes to styling, the new RX-7 has a look that is in keeping with the pure sports car goal Mazda set. Although wheelbase and overall length are within a whisker of the RX-7 it replaces,

ABOVE: The greenhouse portion of the cockpit is much smoother than on the previous RX-7.

BELOW: Striking rear light and spoiler treatment on the 1993 RX-7.

the new car is three inches (7.6cm) wider and an inch (2.5cm) lower. The overall look is one of a no-nonsense coupé.

The front end is derived from the rounded nose found on Mazda's Miata, but with a more aggressive shark-like mouth for engine cooling. Pop-up headlights help keep the nose smooth when they're not in use, and the bonnet has no bulges or scoops to spoil the lines. The sides are also smooth, with the exception of a C-shaped vent that aids cooling of the front brakes. The five-spoke alloy wheels have a very functional look to them, enhanced by the exposed bolt pattern.

The two most striking design elements of the RX-7 are its cockpit and rear. The cockpit compartment has an almost bubble-like look to it, and accentuates the smooth nose and sides. Gone is the large humpback glass rear hatch of the old car. At the rear, the new RX-7 has a glass hatch that slopes more sharply backwards from the peak roofline and flows into an upswept tail.

Across the back of the tail is an integrated rear-light spoiler arrangement that uses a blacked-out insert to tie the rear lights together.

Inside the RX-7, the interior follows the current driver-pod design found on a number of sports cars. A large rev counter is in the centre of the gauge cluster, with a speedometer to the right. Three gauges for fuel level, oil pressure and engine temperature are to the left of the rev counter.

Controls for the air-conditioning and stereo are at the top of a console that sweeps down from the driver's right and connects to the gear box. The steering wheel is adjustable and contains an air-bag supplementary restraint system.

At the start, only a coupé will be offered in the RX-7, meaning an end to the snazzy convertible. The new car will be offered in only two levels – a touring version, with appropriate cockpit upgrading, and a performance-oriented R-1 package, with higher-speed-rated tyres and suspension modifications.

BELOW: Vents just behind the front wheel help keep the RX-7's disc brakes cool.

SPECIFICATIONS

DIMENSIONS

Wheelbase: 95.5in (242.57cm)
Overall length: 168.5in (428cm)
Width: 68.9in (175cm)
Height: 48.4in (123cm)
Front Track: 57.7in (146.5cm)
Rear Track: 57.7in (146.5cm)
Weight: 2,789lb (1,265kg)
Fuel capacity: 20.0gall (75.7l)

ENGINE

Two-Rotor Mazda 13B-STT Wankel
Twin intercooled turbochargers
Bosch D-Jetronic electronic fuel injection
Displacement per rotor: 654cc
Overall displacement: 1308cc
Compression Ratio: 9.0:1
Horsepower: Net 255bhp @ 6500rpm
Torque: Net 217lb-ft @ 5000rpm
Redline: 7000rpm

GEARBOX

Five-speed manual overdrive
Gear ratios: (1) 3.48 (2) 2.01 (3) 1.39 (4) 1.00
(5) 0.71
Rear end ratio: 4.10:1

SUSPENSION

Four-wheel independent
Double wishbone front and rear
Coil springs front and rear
Gas-filled shocks
Front and rear anti-roll bars

STEERING

Power-assisted rack and pinion
Turns, lock-to-lock: 2.9
Turning circle: 35.4ft (10.79m)

BRAKES

Power-assisted four-wheel discs with anti-lock
Disc size: 11.6in (29.46cm) front, 11.6in
(29.46cm) rear

WHEELS AND TYRES

Cast aluminium wheels, 16×8.0in (40.64×
20.32cm), front and rear
225/50ZR steel-belted radials, front and rear

Price was still uncertain prior to its introduction in April 1992, but was expected to be in the $30,000 (£16,925) range.

With its competitors opting to go the more sophisticated route, the new RX-7 could have a clear field. Performance should be astounding, with zero-to-60mph (96.5kmh) times in the five-second range and a top speed of at least 150mph (241kmh). And all of that thanks to Felix Wankel's little engine that goes round and round instead of up and down.

TOP: Leather seats are part of the Touring package on the RX-7.

ABOVE: The cockpit reflects the simple, two-seat sports car theme of the new RX-7.

RIGHT: A full pod of gauges sits directly in front of the driver.

What if you took Japan's top sports cars and tried to make them better? That's just the question a band of California hot rodders and racers asked themselves, and their answers are simply wild.

日本スポーツカー　HOT RODS

日本のスポーツカー

RIGHT: Side skirts and a new front end spoiler accent the Racing Beat RX-7 convertible.

No matter how technologically advanced or refined a sports car may be, there is always a band of experimenters who will try to make improvements on the factory product. For instance, at Porsche there are decades of experience behind each and every car, yet after-market tuners such as Ruf have been able to build modified Porsches that are significantly faster. The German firm of AMG has been building hotter Mercedes-Benzes for nearly two decades, and the firm of Koenig has been improving Ferraris as well.

As the Japanese sports car has matured, individuals have founded thriving companies dedicated to improving cars that at first sight seem close to being perfect. It is not merely coincidence that these firms are mostly based in Southern California, which gave birth to the American hot rod movement in the 1940s and 1950s. California, more than any other place outside Japan, has taken the Japanese sports car to heart, displacing the once dominant German and British marques.

On just about every street there are 300ZXs, Miatas, RX-7s and 3000GTs galore. Because they are so common, there is a natural tendency on the part of some owners to own cars that retain

BELOW: RX-7 modified by Racing Beat topped 238mph (383kph) at the Bonneville Salt Flats.

the Japanese virtues but are just a bit different.

Some of the modified Rising Sun sports cars involve cosmetic changes; from fancier wheels, to spoilers, to wider fenders. Still more involve engine and suspension changes that significantly improve performance. Perhaps the wildest of the modified Japanese sports cars comes from the shops of IMSA racer Steve Millen in Santa Ana, California. Millen, a New Zealander, has an impressive list of racing credentials, including off-track truck racing victories, stints at Le Mans in Nissan's R90CK Group C car, and a string of US wins behind the wheel of Nissan Performance Technology Incorporated's 300ZX.

When the new 300ZX made its debut, Millen set about creating the ultimate ZX, a machine that would be at home on the street yet incorpo-

and back. As for the rear suspension, the Super HICAS four-wheel steering unit that comes as standard on the 300ZX Turbo is removed in favour of the fixed unit found on normally aspirated ZXs. The result is that weight is saved and the rear axle ratio is changed from 3.69:1 to 4.08:1.

Brakes are 11.6in (29.5cm) models from Nissan's Skyline Group A racing saloons, and the rotors are drilled for better heat dissipation.

Under the bonnet, Millen uses a variety of features to increase the standard three-litre turbocharged engine to 460 horsepower. In the GTZ, high-flow fuel injectors are installed, as are significantly larger turbochargers and intercoolers. The entire set-up is controlled electronically through a complex system of airflow and turbo wastegate sensors and valves.

BELOW: Steve Millen's 300GTZ joins his race car and a stock Nissan 300ZX.

BOTTOM: Wild fender skirts and air dams are the mark of Millen's modified 300ZX in front of the team transporter.

rate much of what Millen learned from his racing 300ZX. Starting on the outside, Millen dressed up the standard ZX Turbo with a new front air dam, a high rear wing spoiler and special 17in (43.2cm) Elite wheels with Yokohama A008R tyres. Added to that were gill ducts on the fenders just behind the wheel wells. The car's new designation – GTZ – is painted on the doors in script.

Underneath the arresting bodywork is a plethora of changes that make the Millen GTZ handle and accelerate like a racing car. Special progressive rate coil springs replace the stock units, and adjustable Koni and Tokico shock absorbers are added, as are adjustable anti-sway bars front

ABOVE: In designing the top for the Mitsubishi 3000GT/Dodge Stealth convertible, Straman retained a rounded rear window look.

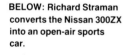

BELOW: Richard Straman converts the Nissan 300ZX into an open-air sports car.

can choose just how wild to make the already formidable 300ZX.

Although not in the performance league of the Steve Millen 300ZX, Southern California coach-maker Richard Straman has his own way of making significant changes to Japanese sports cars – he makes them into convertibles. Working out of a shop in Newport Beach, Straman has more than 20 years of experience in converting cars such as the Mercedes 300CE into an open-air tourer. With the rising popularity of the 300ZX and the Mitsubishi 3000GT VR-4, Straman saw a market for convertible versions.

While it may seem that cutting the roof off a hard-top model is hardly a difficult task, it is not a simple one either. When a roof is removed from most modern cars, the chassis becomes a lot less rigid; on a high-performance sports car, where the engine and suspension put consider-able stress on the chassis and body, increased flex can be fatal. So when the steel roof comes off, Straman adds additional bracing to the car's chassis. In the case of the 300ZX, he retains a roll-bar type hoop behind the front seats to keep the monocoque chassis in place.

In designing a convertible conversion, Straman must also take into account the ease of operation for the soft-top and how the car will look with the top up or down. On the Mitsubishi and Nissan conversions, Straman has achieved a top-up look

Controls that allow the driver to adjust turbo-charger action – including pumping the boost to an amazing 19psi – reside in a control panel that fits inside the stock 300ZX glove box. In addition, a special exhaust system and a beefier clutch are also included.

In its most extreme state of tuning, the Millen GTZ is a rocket, hitting 60mph (96.5kmh) in just 5 seconds and reaching a maximum speed of about 165mph (265.5kmh). Handling is improved to the point the GTZ can hold its own with many racing cars, yet is still versatile enough to be at home on city streets.

A fully modified GTZ would cost nearly $20,000 (£11,765) above the $34,000 (£20,000) base price of a 300ZX, and as an added bonus, Millen offers all of the pieces individually so a customer

that doesn't involve yards and yards of unattractive cloth. When the tops are lowered electrically, they fold down nearly flat and are concealed under a soft boot.

Converting a hard-top to a convertible isn't cheap – $10,500 (£6,175) for the 300ZX Nissan and $14,000 (£8,235) for the Mitsubishi 3000GT VR-4 – but it is one sure way of changing the character of a car. The wind-in-your-face feeling of driving a convertible is enhanced in the 300ZX and the 3000GT VR-4 by the sounds of the multi-valve engines and the tuned exhausts – great noises that are communicated more directly to the driver when the top is down.

The top-down experience is one of the strong selling points of the Mazda MX-5 Miata, but several after-market tuning companies have found ways to increase the appeal of the

extremely popular two-seater. The company Racing Beat, which has had considerable experience racing Mazdas in IMSA, NHRA and Bonneville Salt Flat competition, found the Miata a natural candidate for its performance tweaks. The Anaheim, California, company offers suspension pieces, wider wheels, spoilers and other things to improve the Miata's appearance and handling.

Under the bonnet, Racing Beat offers tuned exhaust headers, fuel injection modifications, more radical camshafts and more efficient cylinder heads to increase the Miata's standard 116

INSET: Racing Beat offers a modified version of the popular Mazda Miata.

BELOW: A deep front air dam and added driving lights are part of the Racing Beat Miata package.

OPPOSITE: Suspension modifications by Racing Beat lower the stock Miata by about 1in (2.5cm).

LEFT: A street RX-7 convertible, right, sits next to an RX-7 modified by Racing Beat.

horsepower. All of this adds some bite to a car that is very well balanced, but lacks some of the power that many people have come to expect from a sports oar.

It's a tribute to the Miata's flexibility that it handles these modifications with few complaints. To see just how far the Miata can be taken, the engineers at Rod Millen Motorsport – Rod is the brother of Steve Millen, who offers the hot rod 300ZX – took the modifications to the limit. Drawing from Rod Millen's experience as a Mazda rally driver, the engineers at Millen's Huntington Beach, California, works decided the Miata could stand a little turbocharging. They lifted the camshafts, pistons, turbocharger, intercooler and radiator from Millen's Mazda 323 GTX rally car and fitted them to the Miata. With a little ingenious tinkering under the Miata's bonnet, the package fitted perfectly.

The result was an engine that cranks out 230 horsepower, nearly double the stock engine's output. That moved the Miata's acceleration into supercar range, with 0 to 60mph (96.5kmh) times of just over 6 seconds – more than 3 seconds faster than a stock MX-5.

The stock Miata gear box was left intact, though the clutch and rear differential were exchanged for heftier versions. Brakes also were changed, with the Millen Miata getting the 10.9in (27.7cm) discs developed for the RX-7 Turbo.

Handling was improved by the installation of thicker anti-sway bars front and back, stiffer coil springs and the lowering of the car by about an inch (2.5cm) overall.

Wheels were changed to special 15 × 7in (38.1 × 17.8cm) 'Aero' look alloys with 205/50VR-15 Bridgestone Potenza tyres. A spoiler was added to the rear and a hard plastic boot was installed over the convertible top well.

The end result of all this tinkering was a Miata that retains its sweet looks, but has the power of the real supercars.

BELOW: With the addition of a turbocharger, the Wankel engine could propel the first RX-7 to speeds nearing 200mph (321.86kph).

Index

PICTURE CREDITS

t = top, b = bottom, m = middle

3 M Lambert; 6 Andrew Morland; 7 t A Morland, m A Morland; 8 t Honda, b A Morland; 9 Andrew Dee; 10 t M Lambert; 11 b Andrew Dee; 12 Honda; 14 Honda; 15 Honda; 16 t David Kimble, b M Lambert; 17 M Lambert; 18 M Lambert; 19 M Lambert; 20 Honda; 21 M Lambert; 22 t M Lambert, b Honda; 24 Toyota; 26 M Lambert; 27 Toyota; 28 Toyota; 29 t M Lambert, b Toyota; 30 t M Lambert, b Toyota; 31 Toyota; 32–38 Mitsubishi; 39 t Mitsubishi, b Mirco Decet; 40 t Mirco Decet, b Mitsubishi; 41–43 Mitsubishi; 44 Nissan; 46 Nissan; 47 Mirco Decet; 48–9 Mirco Decet, Nissan; 52 Mazda; 54 M Lambert; 55 M Lambert, Mazda; 56 Mazda; 57 M Lambert; 58 M Lambert; 59 t + m M Lambert, b Mazda; 62 Mazda; 64 Mazda; 65 t Mazda; 66–69 Mazda; 74 Straman Co; 75 Racing Beat; 76 Racing Beat.

Where not listed, pictures supplied by the author.